A WEEK IN THE LIFE OF THE
Royal Family

by the staff of The Sunday Express Magazine

Macmillan Publishing Company · New York

Endpapers: (*front*) **A State landau brings the new Greek ambassador to Buckingham Palace to present his credentials;** (*back*) **Children greet Prince Philip on his visit to the RAF base at Brüggen, West Germany.**

Title page picture: **The Royal cypher on the door of a State Rolls Royce.**

Macmillan Publishing Company
866 Third Avenue
New York, NY 10022

Library of Congress No. 83–5428

10 9 8 7 6 5 4 3 2 1

First published in 1983 in Great Britain by
George Weidenfeld and Nicolson Limited
91 Clapham High Street, London SW4 7TA

Designed and picture edited by Tony Garrett

Edited by Lynn Barber and Stephen Clackson

Separations by Newsele Litho Ltd
Typeset and bound by Butler & Tanner Ltd,
Frome and London
Printed in Great Britain by Redwood Burn Ltd

CONTENTS

Red carpets are laid wherever the Royal Family goes – this one is for the Queen's visit to the Royal College of Defence Studies. But Prince Philip once said, 'The man who invented the red carpet needed his head examining.'

PREFACE

It was just an ordinary week in the life of the Royal Family: the Queen held a diplomatic reception, Prince Philip paid a flying visit to the British troops in Germany, Prince Charles was in the industrial north, the Princess of Wales was at a children's hospital, and the 'lesser' members of the family were involved in their usual assortment of activities, from singing in a choir to driving a racing car. Between them they clocked up more than eighty royal engagements, the majority of which went unreported in the national press and television.

The idea from which this book grew was a simple one. Despite the great upsurge of public interest in the Royal Family, the media's concentration on just one of its members – the Princess of Wales – was growing increasingly obsessive. So the *Sunday Express Magazine* hit on a device which would reveal a more rounded picture. A week was selected at random (in fact a week in November 1982) and fifteen distinguished magazine writers were commissioned to cover every single royal event in that time.

The results were fascinating. Though three of them had previously written books on royal matters, the normal work of our writers was far removed from the royal 'beat'. All, therefore, brought a fresh and observant eye to the member of the Royal Family they had been assigned to report. Even the most sceptical of them were at once impressed and intrigued by the glimpses they got of the royal way of life.

Putting their reports together, we realized we had constructed a colourful and revealing mosaic of Royalty in action. By simply watching and chronicling every public (and occasionally private) moment in seven days of these very busy lives, we had a composite view as penetrating as anything arrived at by, shall we say, less approved methods. We had also been able to analyse the differing styles of the 'royals', observe how hard they work (very!) and report how cost-effective they are when measured against the public money they receive each year.

This book offers a much expanded version of the material originally published, with great success, in the *Sunday Express Magazine*. Further general background has been added by the magazine's resident columnist and noted royal biographer, Anthony Holden. He points out that it is only in the present reign that the Royal Family has begun to move so freely and so often among ordinary people. The new royal accessibility which this book records, this feeling of the crown inching closer to the people, while remaining, as it must, a revered and lofty symbol, may prove to be Elizabeth II's most important legacy to her subjects.

Ron Hall,
Editor, Sunday Express Magazine

Line of Succession

The Order of Succession

1 Prince Charles
2 Prince William
3 Prince Andrew
4 Prince Edward
5 Princess Anne
6 Peter Phillips
7 Zara Phillips
8 Princess Margaret
9 Viscount Linley
10 Lady Sarah Armstrong-Jones
11 Duke of Gloucester
12 Earl of Ulster
13 Lady Davina Windsor
14 Lady Rose Windsor
15 Duke of Kent
16 Earl of St Andrews
17 Lord Nicholas Windsor
18 Lady Helen Windsor
19 Lord Frederick Windsor*
20 Lady Gabriella Windsor*
21 Princess Alexandra
22 James Ogilvy
23 Marina Ogilvy
24 Earl of Harewood
25 Viscount Lascelles
26 Alexander Lascelles
27 Hon. James Lascelles
28 Rowan Lascelles
29 Sophie Lascelles
30 Hon. Robert Lascelles
31 Hon. Gerald Lascelles
32 Henry Lascelles
33 Duke of Fife
34 Earl of Macduff
35 Lady Alexandra Carnegie
36 King Olav of Norway
37 Crown Prince Harald of Norway
38 Prince Haakon of Norway
39 Princess Martha of Norway
40 Princess Ragnhild, Mrs Lorentzen
41 Haakon Lorentzen
42 Ingeborg Lorentzen
43 Ragnhild Lorentzen
44 Princess Astrid, Mrs Ferner
45 Alexander Ferner
46 Carl Christian Ferner
47 Cathrine Ferner
48 Benedicte Ferner
49 Elisabeth Ferner
50 Princess Margarita of Romania

QUEEN VICTORIA
1819–1901
m. Prince Albert of Saxe Coburg
and Gotha (Prince Consort)

* Prince Michael of Kent gave up his right to the
succession on his marriage to a Roman Catholic. Their
children (19, 20), however, remain on the list. Any other
children born to Prince Charles and Princess Diana will
follow Prince William in the order of succession - other
sons preceding daughters regardless of age.

6

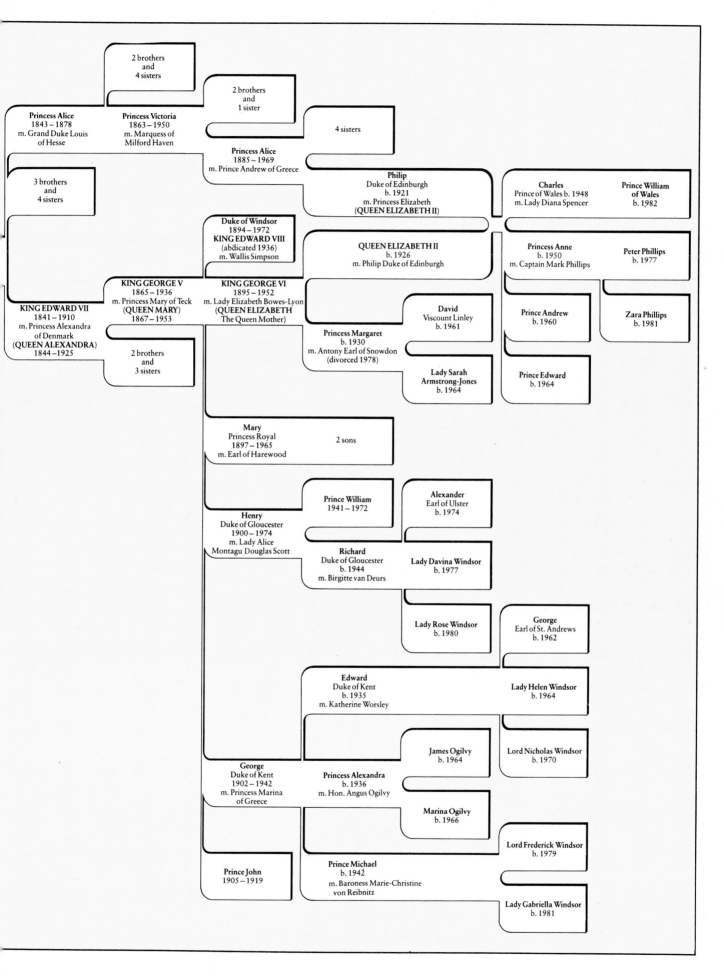

Princess Alice
1843 – 1878
m. Grand Duke Louis
of Hesse

Princess Victoria
1863 – 1950
m. Marquess of
Milford Haven

2 brothers
and
4 sisters

2 brothers
and
1 sister

4 sisters

Princess Alice
1885 – 1969
m. Prince Andrew of Greece

Philip
Duke of Edinburgh
b. 1921
m. Princess Elizabeth
(QUEEN ELIZABETH II)

Charles
Prince of Wales b. 1948
m. Lady Diana Spencer

Prince William
of Wales
b. 1982

3 brothers
and
4 sisters

Duke of Windsor
1894 – 1972
KING EDWARD VIII
(abdicated 1936)
m. Wallis Simpson

QUEEN ELIZABETH II
b. 1926
m. Philip Duke of Edinburgh

Princess Anne
b. 1950
m. Captain Mark Phillips

Peter Phillips
b. 1977

KING EDWARD VII
1841 – 1910
m. Princess Alexandra
of Denmark
(QUEEN ALEXANDRA)
1844 – 1925

KING GEORGE V
1865 – 1936
m. Princess Mary of Teck
(QUEEN MARY)
1867 – 1953

KING GEORGE VI
1895 – 1952
m. Lady Elizabeth Bowes-Lyon
(QUEEN ELIZABETH
The Queen Mother)

Princess Margaret
b. 1930
m. Antony Earl of Snowdon
(divorced 1978)

David
Viscount Linley
b. 1961

Prince Andrew
b. 1960

Zara Phillips
b. 1981

Lady Sarah
Armstrong-Jones
b. 1964

Prince Edward
b. 1964

2 brothers
and
3 sisters

Mary
Princess Royal
1897 – 1965
m. Earl of Harewood

2 sons

Henry
Duke of Gloucester
1900 – 1974
m. Lady Alice
Montagu Douglas Scott

Prince William
1941 – 1972

Alexander
Earl of Ulster
b. 1974

Richard
Duke of Gloucester
b. 1944
m. Birgitte van Deurs

Lady Davina Windsor
b. 1977

Lady Rose Windsor
b. 1980

George
Earl of St. Andrews
b. 1962

Edward
Duke of Kent
b. 1935
m. Katherine Worsley

Lady Helen Windsor
b. 1964

James Ogilvy
b. 1964

Lord Nicholas Windsor
b. 1970

George
Duke of Kent
1902 – 1942
m. Princess Marina
of Greece

Princess Alexandra
b. 1936
m. Hon. Angus Ogilvy

Marina Ogilvy
b. 1966

Lord Frederick Windsor
b. 1979

Prince John
1905 – 1919

Prince Michael
b. 1942
m. Baroness Marie-Christine
von Reibnitz

Lady Gabriella Windsor
b. 1981

BEHIND THE SCENES

A landau sets out from the Royal Mews to bring the new Greek Ambassador to Buckingham Palace. There are some seventy-odd carriages in the Mews, with thirty horses to pull them and forty grooms and coachmen to look after them. The top horses are the Windsor Grays, which always pull the Queen's carriage; lesser dignitaries are pulled by bays. At least one carriage goes out from the Mews every day, to run errands around London and exercise the horses.

Around the Garden Door at the rear of Buckingham Palace hovers a charmed circle of distinguished-looking men, making discreet small talk in politely hushed tones. They shift frequently from foot to foot, and cast regular, rather anxious looks at their watches. Footmen in tails and maroon waistcoats come and go, bringing news of the sovereign's progress through the private apartments above.

A twenty-year-old Rolls-Royce Phantom v, devoid either of number-plates or outside handles on its rear doors, draws up beside the scene; an anonymous-looking figure, who is in fact a senior policeman, unlocks the rear door from inside and holds it open in readiness. A painted shield bearing the Royal coat of arms is attached to a clip on the front of the roof.

These are regular rituals when the monarch is in London, yet there is still among this privileged and very formal group of men a keen sense of anticipation, almost nervousness.

A door opens a few feet away, seemingly of its own accord, and there emerges a small, neatly dressed figure who passes quickly, almost imperceptibly, between their bowed heads and into the car. Two private secretaries and a lady-in-waiting climb in after her. The detective closes the door, jumps into the front seat, and they are gone. The inner circle continues to hover respectfully for a moment, watching the stately progress of the disappearing Rolls, then disperses back to its desks around the Palace. Queen Elizabeth ii has left home for another official engagement.

The group will reassemble beside the Garden Door an hour or two later to greet its mistress' return, and to inquire politely if all passed off according to plan. The answer is invariably yes – apart from a passing joke, perhaps, about a nervous dignitary or a dropped bouquet – for the outing has been meticulously planned by these very people. The Queen's close circle of advisers will always have trodden her every step in advance of her, will know the names of those to whom she has been introduced, will have met those people beforehand and briefed them on how to behave. Never, for instance, never extend your hand to shake the monarch's; wait for the Royal glove to be extended towards you. Such is the stuff of life on Her Majesty's Service.

The Queen undertakes some four hundred public engagements a year, and the Royal Family between them some two thousand. Going out and about, seeing and being seen, bestowing their favour on British organizations and activities and their smiles on the British people: all this is perhaps their principal function these days. It is only in this century, since the reign of King Edward vii, that the monarchy has begun to move among its people to quite this extent. Elizabeth ii, who has altered the monarchy's role in a number of subtle ways, has always placed great emphasis on this kind of royal patronage: it is one of the ways in which she has consciously brought the monarchy closer to its people, while taking care to preserve the essential, almost mystical gulf between the two.

The Queen has certainly travelled more of the world than any British sovereign before her, but she has also travelled more of her own kingdom. She has a fleet of seven official cars, a train, a yacht, three aeroplanes, and two helicopters in which to do so. It is official Palace policy that the monarch does not fly by helicopter unless it is essential (as, for instance, on her last visit to Northern Ireland), so she is the most frequent user of the specially-equipped Royal train, which has all the latest in photocopying and other such office equipment as well as the domestic conveniences necessary for long journeys and overnight stops. The Prince of Wales has also proved himself fond of the train, though he and his father of course enjoy flying themselves around in the three thirty-year-old twin turbo-prop Andovers which, with two Westland Wessex HC4 helicopters and a staff of 140 RAF personnel, constitute the Queen's Flight.

All these modes of transport are available to the dozen or so other Royals who earn their annual income from the Civil List (see the chart on page 11) by undertaking regular engagements on behalf of the nation's and the Commonwealth's first family. The planning of the public work of what King George VI called 'the family firm' is surprisingly unco-ordinated. Contrary to popular belief, there is no annual general meeting at which the demands of the months ahead are distributed around the family. Royal cousins or siblings have even been known to bump into each other unexpectedly while on duty in far-flung corners of the realm.

Each member of the family has his or her own private secretary or staff with whom they sit down several times a year to go through the multitude of requests for their presence. In the Prince of Wales's office, for instance, there is a map of Britain with several layers of plastic overlay indicating the regions he has recently visited, to ensure an even geographical spread of his royal favours. Whether or not an invitation is accepted is very much a matter of whether or not the Royal in question thinks it a worthy cause, or one which appeals to some quirk in his range of personal interests. Rarely can staff persuade a member of the Royal Family to do something or go somewhere against his or her will.

Most groups and organizations hoping for a Royal visit make the mistake of writing to the Palace and asking for 'a member of the Royal Family' to come and bless their endeavours. All such letters – the vast majority – are returned with a polite request that you decide which member of the Royal Family you want, and write directly to them. As one official put it privately: 'We are not in the business of rent-a-royal.' There is no general committee meeting at which appointments are parcelled out.

Once a decision has been made in your favour, you will receive a delegation from the Palace to go over the arrangements with you in immense detail. It's not just a question of hiring a red carpet and teaching the chairman's granddaughter to curtsey: there are countless details of which you will not have thought (quite apart from submitting a draft guest list for vetting at the Palace). How many hands do you expect the Royal personage to shake? How far do you expect him or her to walk? How much time have you allotted for this as opposed to that? Do you seriously expect Princess Anne to walk through there without roping that bit off? Have you discussed security with the local police? Have you arranged all the necessary, er, conveniences? Did you know that Prince Charles doesn't care for red wine, and prefers coffee to tea, but always reserves the right to change his mind? Will any food be offered – and if so, what – and did you know that no photographs may ever be taken of the Royal Family eating or drinking? Talking of the press, may I introduce my colleague, Her Majesty's assistant press secretary ..., and perhaps this is the moment to explain the workings of the royal Press rota.

Etc, etc. Cameras, both press and private, will come in for detailed discussion, as they are a vexed issue at present. Not merely do the Royals get tired of having lenses poked in their faces while they try to talk to people; they are deeply aware that many who have been waiting hours to see them, often in the cold or the rain, may have their view obscured at the last minute by a rampant mob of press photographers. This was one of the items on the agenda when national newspaper editors were summoned to the Palace last year over the intense harassment of the Princess of Wales.

Occasionally, of course, you may get a surprise letter from a Royal personage suggesting that *they* visit *you*. Each member of the family tends to specialize in certain areas of interest, which are reflected by the places and the people on whom they like to drop in. A few sporting examples illustrate just how random the whole business can be. The Queen, for instance, finds tennis boring, so the annual duty of bestowing the Royal blessing on Wimbledon has been inherited by the Duke and Duchess of Kent from his late mother, Princess Marina. Few of the Royal Family are football fans, so whoever is on duty, with some reluctance, in those two FA Cup Final seats so coveted by Her Majesty's loyal subjects is likely to have been volunteered – on the Buggins' Turn principle – from the ranks of the 'minor Royals'. And no Windsor since King Edward VIII, later the Duke of Windsor, has shown the slightest interest in golf – a sport which in this reign has suffered conspicuous royal neglect.

The newest arrival, the Princess of Wales, seems likely for now to corner the market in kindergartens and tap-dancing. Her husband underwent a crash course in government and industry during the couple of years before their wedding, organized for him by the National Economic Development Office. 'Neddy', in its corporate wisdom, decided he should specialize in fork-lift trucks, with the result that in 1978-79 such firms as Hyster (Europe) Ltd in Scotland, Coventry Climax in the Midlands and Lansing Bagnall in Basingstoke, Hants, were the proud recipients of unsolicited princely visits. Quite apart from excitement enough to reduce hardened tycoons to tears, a photo of the Prince of Wales at the wheel of their latest model can do wonders for the order book, both at home and abroad.

The longer and more distant the trip, of course, the greater the logistics involved. An overseas tour on the scale of the Queen's four-week visit this year to the Cayman Islands, Jamaica, California and Canada will involve more luggage than most of us will take abroad in our lifetimes. But even in the more remote reaches of the British Isles, any of the senior Royal Family will carry with them, for instance, a full set

The Civil List

The Queen	£3,704,217
Prince Philip	£171,100
Princess Anne	£106,500
Prince Andrew	£20,000*
Prince Edward	£16,183
Queen Mother	£306,600
Princesss Margaret	£104,500
Princess Alice	£42,000
Duke of Gloucester	£83,900
Duke of Kent	£113,000
Princess Alexandra	£42,000
Total	£4,710,000

These figures are for 1982-83; they are updated annually. The last increase, in March 1982, represented an eight per cent rise. The Queen has had no personal allowance from the Civil List since 1971 – taking her private expenditure from her own income. This includes the tax-free revenue of the Duchy of Lancaster estates which last year was £1,075,000. The size of her investments has never been revealed, but they include a substantial stock portfolio.

More than three-quarters of the costs of official royal duties are met by the taxpayer beyond the Civil List – this includes the upkeep of the *Britannia* (£3.4 million), the Queen's Flight (£2.7 million – on the defence budget with the Royal Yacht), the Royal Train (£400,000 – met by British Rail) and the upkeep of the Royal Palaces – Buckingham Palace, Windsor Castle, St James's Palace, Kensington Palace and Hampton Court (£7,461,000, administered by the Department of the Environment). The Queen maintains Sandringham and Balmoral herself.

Prince Charles is not on the Civil List, benefiting instead from the tax-free revenues of the Duchy of Cornwall, giving a quarter of that money to the state in lieu of tax (it was half until his marriage). In 1981 he kept £580,000 of the £771,000 Duchy profits.

The Queen refunded £300,000 in 82/83 to cover the Civil List payments to the Gloucesters, Kents, and Princess Alexandra. All told, it can be reliably estimated that the overall cost to the country of the Monarchy is in excess of £18.5 million.

of mourning clothes, in case of an untimely royal death elsewhere. Crates of signed and framed photographs – the splendour of the frame indexed to the grandeur of the recipient – are carried everywhere as gifts. On journeys of this scale, at least one valet (or dresser), a baggage master and other such ancillary staff will join the standard retinue of private secretaries, press secretaries, equerries (or ladies-in-waiting), detectives and transport staff.

When the Royal Family are on official visits abroad, they are designated quasi-Ambassadors for Britain, and so the costs are borne by a special department of the Foreign Office. At home, travelling costs are one of the heavy financial burdens relieved by the Civil List. The Prince of Wales is not on the Civil List: his income comes from his Duchy of Cornwall estates. Out of this substantial amount (averaging some £771,000 a year before he surrenders a quarter as voluntary income tax), he must also pay the salaries of his staff, from private secretary to stable boy.

There are 346 full-time staff in Buckingham Palace, the vast majority of whom are on the Queen's own Household budget rather than the state's. They are never going to get rich in the Royal employ, but they lead a pleasantly grand life in large offices with Old Masters on the wall, taking tea from antique silver teapots served by liveried flunkeys. Visitors to the palace are often surprised by the dowdiness of its furnishing; the ancient central heating system is notoriously cranky, many a carpet is worn through to the floorboards and there are always a number of rooms overdue for redecoration. King Edward VIII, after his abdication, referred to the Palace as 'a sepulchre', saying that 'its stately rooms and endless corridors and passages ... seemed pervaded by a curious musty smell. I was never happy there.'

The atmosphere in fact resembles that of an ancient university, the visitor often feeling rather like a pupil to the donnish private secretary sitting behind his large desk in his huge, untidy room. There is also a strict hierarchy. The most powerful person in the palace, apart from the monarch herself, is the Queen's private secretary, Sir Philip Moore, a sixty-one-year-old ex-

Royalty on the move needs a staggering quantity of luggage. The Queen never travels anywhere without her feather pillows, her hot-water bottle, her monogrammed electric kettle. Once when the Duchess of Windsor came to England she brought thirty-five pieces of luggage. Her secretary explained that this was 'just an ordinary wardrobe for a week's stay.'

The Queen Mother has been in the Royal business for longer than anyone else. She became a Royal in 1923 when she married the then Duke of York, and now, at eighty-three, she is the oldest surviving member of the Royal Family. Yet, despite her age, she carried out 115 official engagements last year, and shows no inclination to retire.

diplomat and former England rugby international. It is with Sir Philip and his deputy, Australian-born Sir William Heseltine, that Her Majesty will sift through the innumerable requests for her presence. When a visit is agreed, one of them will be joined on what they call the 'recce' by the Queen's press secretary, Michael Shea, another former diplomat who also writes novels (and managed in 1981 to publish three books as well as handle the press arrangements for the Royal Wedding).

The Prince of Wales has a similar support staff in the portly shape of his private secretary, Edward Adeane, a barrister who gave up his practice to follow three generations of his family into the Royal service, and a small private office. His public relations are looked after by two assistant press secretaries, one of them always a Commonwealth diplomat on temporary secondment, who also try to persuade the Duke of Edinburgh to be a little kinder to journalists. The Duke has his own private secretary, as indeed does the Princess of Wales, who inherited one of the younger high-flyers, another FO man named Oliver Everett, from her husband.

Public interest in the Royal Family has grown into such an obsession these last few years that life for the Palace staff is mightily busy when their employers are in London. But there are, of course, long 'down periods', when the Queen retires from public engagements: six weeks at Windsor and Sandringham at Christmas and New Year, four at Windsor at Easter, and ten at Balmoral in late summer and early autumn. Her work as a monarch goes on – keeping up with the daily boxes of state papers, signing legislation, dealing with a vast correspondence – but for the rest of the family, the year contains long breaks. They are always seen to be working hard when about the business of the family firm, but the firm rewards them with longer holidays than most.

They may lack the flair of Madison Avenue, but the combination of the Queen as chairman and her successive private secretaries as managing director has proved itself adept at public relations over the thirty-one years of her reign. Many Royal activities we now take for granted – the 'walkabout', for instance – are in fact Elizabeth II's personal innovations. The turning-point was the television film 'Royal Family', made in 1969 to mark the investiture of the Prince of Wales at Caernarvon. For the first time in history, the British people saw their Royal Family in private – and realized that they were after all quite like the rest of us, capable of shouting at each other and burning the toast. When the ceremony was televised the morning after the film was shown, the hands that placed the crown on Prince Charles's head had last been seen wielding a barbecue fork.

It is still less than fifty years since the abdication of the Queen's uncle brought the British monarchy to its knees. Many Labour politicians, and a surprisingly high percentage of the nation, saw the events of 1936 as an opportune moment to do away with the institution of monarchy. Elizabeth II now sees it as her and her father's central achievement to have restored the crown, in a comparatively short period, to as secure and stable a popularity as at any time in its long history. She herself was surprised by the strength of the national rejoicing at her Silver Jubilee in 1977; and that success has now been enhanced by the events of the last two years, in which the marriage of the Prince of Wales and the birth of his son Prince William have at last brought the next generation of her family to the fore.

And the particular magic of monarchy, to a nation which now seems to relish it as a therapy for its other voluminous troubles, depends in large degree on these public appearances: on monarchy made flesh. The British will never want their Royals to go Scandanavian, to get jobs in offices and join them on commuter transport. It is a delicate balance. But in moving more among her people, while keeping a proper distance the rest of the time, the Queen has resecured her family's foundations. By the time her son succeeds her, more of their subjects all over the world will have seen, shaken hands with, talked to these two British monarchs than any of their predecessors. It is an achievement for which history will remember her.
Anthony Holden

The Queen's Homes

The Royal Yacht *Britannia* (right) is used for royal honeymoons and as a base for state visits abroad. Launched in 1954 at a cost of £2 million, her décor is described by its designer, Sir Hugh Casson, as 'a restrained English country-house style'. The ship's running costs are met by the Ministry of Defence, and the ship is at the disposal of the Admiralty when not in royal use. But she was not sent to the Falklands because of difficulties in fuelling.

The Royal Family changed its name to Windsor in 1917 to mark its long association with Windsor Castle (below. Here Prince Philip drives a four-in-hand through the Great Park.) It is the oldest of the Royal residences, and also the most costly to run – about £3½ million a year. It has its own police station, swimming pool, and nuclear fallout shelter. The Royal Family always spends Christmas, Easter and Ascot week at Windsor.

Sandringham (above) is the Queen's favourite home and she traditionally spends New Year there with her family. It is an enormous pile of no architectural distinction standing among 20,000 windswept acres. Most of the blackcurrants that go into Ribena are grown there, and the Queen's racing pigeon loft is nearby, at King's Lynn. An Edwardian Lady of the Bedchamber said it would be hard to imagine 'a more ugly and desolate place'. Yet successive monarchs have loved it, not least for its first-rate shooting which, in Edwardian times, produced average bags of 30,000 head each season. The present Queen has struggled in vain to 'rationalize' Sandringham. In the mid-1970s she approved plans to demolish 91 of its 274 rooms, but, after three years' work and an outlay of over £20,000, she called a halt. The gardens of Sandringham are open to the public in the summer.

The bit of Buckingham Palace (above) that one sees from the Mall is only a fraction of the whole vast edifice designed by John Nash. It contains more rooms than anyone has ever been able to count, as well as a post office, telephone exchange, swimming pool, nuclear fallout shelter and operating theatre. It is reputedly connected to the London Underground by a secret branch line. None of its occupants has ever had a good word to say for it. Edward VII called it 'a sepulchre', George VI 'an icebox', and Princess Diana wrote to a friend soon after her engagement, 'Life at Buckingham Palace isn't too bad, but too many formal dinners (Yuk!)'

Balmoral (left) in the Highlands, is the Royal Family's summer holiday home. It was built by Queen Victoria as 'a pretty little castle in the old Scotch style', but her son, Edward VII, called it 'the Highland Barn of 1000 Draughts'. Prince Charles is a keen Balmoral fan and his children's book *The Old Man of Loch-na-Gar* is named after the local mountain, but Princess Diana fled early from her first holiday there. The main attractions of Balmoral are its prime fishing and its grouse moors.

Several of the shops in Ballater (below) carry the Royal Warrant, it being the nearest town to Balmoral. This one is the baker's, George Leith. The royal milk (bottom) is delivered three times a week from the royal dairy farms at Windsor, in special bottles with the Queen's gold monogram on the tops. The Queen is reputed to have said that it was seeing her cypher on the milk that first convinced her she was Queen.

THE QUEEN

Sunday
Windsor Castle

Monday
To Buckingham Palace at midday. Mrs Thatcher reports for her weekly one-hour meeting at 6.30 pm.

Tuesday
Various audiences including our new Ambassador to Vietnam, a retiring Air Chief Marshal and the new Greek Ambassador, Nicholas Kyriazides presenting his credentials and members of his staff.
Annual Palace reception for Diplomatic Corps (2,000 guests).

Wednesday
Royal College of Defence Studies. Board of Deputies of British Jews reception, St James's Palace.

Thursday
To Sandringham for the Retriever Championships field trials.

Friday
Retriever Championships continue.
To the Kent home of Lord and Lady Brabourne, with Prince Philip and Prince Andrew.

Off-duty at Sandringham, the Queen awards prizes for the International Gundog League Retriever Field Trials. Her own dog, Sandringham Salt, was unplaced. Presenting an award to the handler who knocked her dog out, the Queen joked: 'I don't think I should be giving you this.'

For the Queen it was a three-day working week, sandwiched between two long country weekends. There were no 'meet the people' walkabouts: instead, there was a tightly-packed programme of official, political and diplomatic engagements all connected with the Monarch's role as head of state. The events of the week had been carefully selected several months beforehand at one of the twice-yearly office staff meetings presided over by the Queen's Private Secretary, Sir Philip Moore.

In their quiet, rather old-fashioned offices in the Palace, the secretarial staff sort and sift the thousands of invitations received by the Queen. They fit the few acceptances possible into the framework of annual and special engagements of state and foreign visits. Bulky dossiers of detail accumulate long before the event.

In between her public engagements the Queen must find time to bring herself up to date on current affairs and one of her most important tasks is the dutiful reading of state papers. These are the famous 'boxes' which used to be brought by royal messenger in a small horse-drawn carriage, and now, more prosaically, in a van from the government offices. Although the Queen is by now an experienced fast reader, she must spend many hours a week digesting papers which are by no means always fascinating reading.

She reads through half-moon glasses at her desk in a high room at the back of the Palace, as often as not kicking off her shoes for comfort. When Parliament is in session she receives a daily report of proceedings prepared by Tory MP Carol Mather and transmitted from the House of Commons by telex.

After a quiet Sunday at Windsor Castle in traditional form – riding, Sunday papers, church, lunch, dogs and television – the Queen returned to Buckingham Palace at midday on Monday to take up her official life. At 6.30 pm she received her weekly visit from the Prime Minister. Earlier in the reign when she had young children the PM's visit was put back so as to give the Queen time to be with her children at tea, and the custom has stuck. What transpired at the meeting remains a state secret: Winston Churchill once confided to his Private Secretary that he spent his time with the Queen talking about racing, but it seems unlikely that Mrs Thatcher does the same.

The Queen had no other engagement that day, so was able to enjoy the luxury of a quiet evening at home alone (Prince Philip being in Germany). She may have spent the time catching up on the personal diary she has kept all her life – a top-secret document seen by none.

Tuesday began as usual with tea in bed, breakfast soon after eight, with the morning papers, *Telegraph* crossword, and personal mail. The Queen's private letters are carefully distinguished from the official mail by initials on the envelopes. When the Duke is at home, they breakfast together, often listening to the BBC News. At 9 am whenever the Queen is in residence, Pipe Major Brian Macrae marches up and down playing the bagpipes – a custom inherited from Queen Victoria, which in the early days of their marriage seemed not entirely

congenial to Prince Philip. The Queen's clothes are laid out by Miss Margaret 'Bobo' MacDonald, who was the Queen's nurserymaid when she was a child and has been her dresser since 1952. (Her sister Ruby was Princess Margaret's dresser until 1961.) She is the Queen's longest-standing servant and enjoys a privileged position in the Household. The Queen's hair is set by Charles Martin from Daniel Neville's, who also accompanies the Royal party on foreign tours.

This particular working morning was spent reading and signing papers with Sir Philip Moore and then receiving official visitors. First to arrive was Mr M. E. Pike, the newly-appointed Ambassador Extraordinary and Plenipotentiary at Hanoi. The Court Circular subsequently reported that he 'kissed hands', but according to a Palace spokesman, the actual kissing is not obligatory on such occasions. Perhaps just

as well, since the Queen's hands come in for a good deal of wear and tear, with handshakes galore on every occasion, often from people who do not understand that protocol demands a limp grasp.

An Air Chief Marshal came to relinquish his appointment at Strike Command of the RAF and a Clerk of the Crown in Chancery came to mark his retirement.

Then the new Greek ambassador with his diplomatic entourage arrived by coach to present his credentials to the Court of St James. Nicholas Kyriazides was led through the Palace to the so-called 1844 Room at the back to be presented to the Queen. The ceremony was a finely wrought compromise between formal – two steps forwards and don't forget to put the left foot first, bow to the Queen – and informal, with a lively and cordial chat afterwards. It was clear that her Majesty was well informed about Greece and that

One of the three State landaus is sent from the Royal Mews to bring the Greek ambassador, Nicholas Kyriazides to Buckingham Palace to present his credentials to the Queen. Officially, ambassadors do not exist until they have 'kissed hands'. In fact the Queen met Mr Kyriazides at a diplomatic reception a few days earlier and, as she left, she said with a smile, 'I haven't met you yet, have I?'

she knew the new ambassador was until recently Deputy Governor of the Central Bank, for the conversation turned upon international economics.

Then the ambassador's wife was presented and there was talk about visiting Scotland. There were friendly words too for the embassy staff and when the most junior, Vassilis Pispinis, came forward the Queen, who stood throughout the 20-minute session, raised a laugh by saying, 'Ah. You must be the one who does all the work.'

On Tuesday evening the Queen held her 'Evening Reception at Buckingham Palace for the Diplomatic Corps' which is generally regarded as the most important occasion of the diplomatic year. Representatives of all the 144 diplomatic missions in London, with wives and daughters, plus British civil servants, members of Government and Opposition, brought the guest list up to two thousand people, all wearing full evening dress.

On duty for the occasion were the

splendidly-attired Bodyguard of the Honourable Corps of Gentlemen-At-Arms, the Queen's Bodyguard of Yeomen of the Guard; and a dismounted detachment of Household Cavalry to line the way in. Police officers of the Royal Protection Group maintained a discreet surveillance.

The Queen's duty schedule allowed for only half a minute to greet each delegation whether it were the Soviet Union or Cyprus. The guests were marshalled in groups according to ambassador's seniority in the White Room, the Blue Room, the Picture Gallery or the Ballroom. As soon as the Royal party had passed through one sector, it was cordoned off by a line of Yeomen of the Guard so that the diplomats there could begin sipping their champagne without further ado.

The Queen came first, the Duke next, clad in his court dress with stockings and silk breeches, and then the Prince and Princess of Wales ('Delightful', everyone agreed), and other Royals.

The Queen and the Duke of Edinburgh set off for the Royal College of Defence Studies in Belgrave Square. The Queen's detective sits beside the driver, and her lady-in-waiting and private secretary follow in the back-up car. The Queen's five State cars, all Rolls Royces, are the only cars in the UK not to carry numberplates.

At the Royal College of Defence Studies, the Queen is greeted by its Commandant, Admiral Sir William Pillar, before being taken in to hear a 40-minute lecture on the future of NATO. The Queen, who trained in the ATS during the war, is always happy among service personnel and, on this occasion, stayed considerably longer than her schedule demanded. Before she arrived preparations at the College included laying sticky tape on the front steps (inset far left) to secure the red carpet.

First to be presented was the Dean of the Diplomatic Corps, Inoke Faletau, High Commissioner for Tonga, resplendent in his national dress. 'The Queen asked me about the Royal family of Tonga whom she knows well,' Mr Faletau reported afterwards. 'She talked about her visit to the South Pacific and said how much she enjoyed it.' Everyone agrees that the Queen is brilliant at talking to diplomats, often displaying considerable knowledge of the countries they represent. She is also consistently helpful to the Foreign Office, putting on lunches and receptions at short notice to gratify distinguished foreign visitors and generally oil the diplomatic wheels. It is part of her job of course, but she does it with signally good grace.

After the Queen had greeted all her guests and withdrawn, the more sprightly diplomats danced to the music of the Coldstream Guards. 'Every one of us must have remembered reading as a child about dancing in a Royal palace, and here it was happening to us,' reported Inoke Faletau. 'Swing was in the air and the music was pretty hot with some New Orleans numbers.'

The Queen meets some of her one million Jewish subjects at a reception organized by the Board of Deputies of British Jews. The reception was held to mark the end of a three-day conference, and the invitation to the Queen was issued a year beforehand. The conference itself was held at a hotel, but the Queen's staff suggested that it might be better to hold the reception in private rooms, and they offered the use of St James's Palace. The Palace rooms are not for hire exactly, but they are occasionally loaned out to approved bodies, as they were in this case.

St James's Palace was the Royal Family's main London residence until Queen Victoria moved the Court to Buckingham Palace. It now houses mainly grace-and-favour apartments, and offices such as the Lord Chamberlain's Department.

A curious feature of this and many other Royal occasions, was that afterwards no-one could describe what the Queen wore. Even trained observers like diplomats' wives were so transfixed by the Queen's blue eyes and regal presence that they could only recall something 'glittering and grand', 'sparkling and magnificent'. In fact, according to the official Palace description, it was 'a dress of fine gold lace, the bodice embroidered with seed pearls and incandescent beads.' With it, she wore a ruby and diamond tiara and the Order of the Garter.

It is perhaps no accident that the Queen's clothes are so unmemorable. Her evening dresses are designed to show off the jewellery and orders which are deemed appropriate for the occasion. Perforce she relies on British designers and she has remained loyal to those couture houses – Hardy Amies, Hartnell, and Hartnell's trainee Ian Thomas (who also designs for Mrs Thatcher) – with whom she started her reign. Her shoes, which must be comfortable rather than elegant, come from Rayne and her hats from Simone Mirman. She is not extravagant. She often wears the same outfit in public many times, only varying the effect with new accessories. After her Saudi Arabian visit, when she had to wear long dresses all the time, she had several of the dresses shortened for day wear so that they should not go to waste. It is striking that almost none of her outfits has been copied for mass consumption (unlike so many of Princess Diana's). The Queen has no ambition to be a style-setter: she probably sees herself as being above fashion in the same way that she is above party politics.

On Wednesday morning just before 11 am two Rolls Royces, one bearing the Royal standard and a St George silver mascot upon its bonnet, made the short journey from Buckingham Palace to Seaford House in Belgrave Square, the home of the Royal College of Defence Studies.

The Queen's detective, Chief Inspector Brian Jeffrey, sprang from his seat beside the chauffeur and the Queen and the Duke of Edinburgh emerged from the back, to be greeted by Admiral Sir William Pillar, Commandant of the College. The second car disgorged two officers-in-attendance, the Duchess of Grafton, and the Queen's Private Secretary. The Queen, in cherry-coloured suit and hat, and the Duke in naval uniform, were led up to the first floor lecture theatre, where three student officers took their places at the lectern to open a 40-minute paper on 'Can the non-communist world survive without NATO?'

The lecture was attended by seventy-six senior officers – Brigadiers or equivalent – from Britain, the Commonwealth and NATO, and the Duke because of his naval background, and the Queen, as Commander-in-Chief of the forces, displayed great interest.

Afterwards members of the college staff were presented. They all had drinks in the ante-room, and the Queen gave every sign of enjoying herself – indeed, staying longer than the programme demanded. Next day a warm letter of thanks arrived promptly from the Palace.

The Queen feels particularly at home with the armed forces, because they provide a well-ordered atmosphere compatible with her own way of life, and because the position of those introduced to

At the end of the Jewish reception, the Queen is presented with a menorah, the seven-branched candelabrum used in the Festival of Lights. What happens to all the presents the Queen receives every year? According to a Palace spokesman, they are all kept – 'The Queen has four very large houses, you know' – though objects of particular ethnic or historical interest may be loaned to appropriate museums.

her is clearly stamped upon them by their badges of rank. How different, how very different, from civilians who often seem to be dressed alike and whose degree of importance is more difficult to distinguish.

After lunch at the Palace the Queen was not on duty in public, though she must have been conscious of the ceremony taking place upon the lawns at the back as battalions of the Scots Guards and Welsh Guards, and troops of the Blues and Royals marched in to receive the South Atlantic Medals they had earned in the Falklands Campaign.

By 6 pm there was already a queue of guests at the reception organized by the Board of Deputies of British Jews at St James's Palace, the older and more compact Royal Palace in London. The numerous Rolls Royces drawing into Friary Court were of noticeably more recent vintage than those which transported the Queen and the Duke of Edinburgh half an hour later.

'Don't crowd the Queen', cried Sgt Philips, the ramrod superintendent of the State Apartments. Peter Hartley, the Assistant Secretary of the Lord Chamberlain's office, preceded the Royals, politely but firmly pressing back the throng. Suddenly a camera flashed at the Queen when it should not have done. Her eyes, very blue, registered her reactions sure and true as those of a great actress – surprise, a flash of real momentary anger, fast transformed into a warm smile.

'I'm terribly sorry, Ma'am. It was my editor', apologized the man from *The Jewish Chronicle*.

'Some people have influence', remarked the Queen in her girlish tone. Everyone laughed and the party moved on, the Queen in a peacock blue cocktail dress, three rows of pearls and jewelled pendant on the shoulder; the Duke in grey suit and sporty shirt, looking younger out of uniform. They were followed by their staff, the Duchess of Grafton, Mistress of the Robes; Sir William Heseltine, Deputy Private Secretary; and the Equerry, Squadron Leader Adam Wise. Further away the two duty detectives moved quietly and vigilantly among the guests drinking Carmel wine and eating kosher canapes.

Handlers and their dogs at Sandringham at the start of the second day of the Gundog League Retriever trials (below). The Queen spent both days enthusiastically following the various events, walking across muddy fields and marshland. Peter Moxon, kennel editor of the *Shooting Times*, said: 'The Queen was absolutely marvellous. She walked everywhere with the competitors. We covered miles and miles and there was no question of a vehicle to pick her up. She was really in her element.'

For an hour the Queen was 'on stage' among her subjects, and the theatrical comparison is apt because to see her entering such a room is like standing in the wings to watch an actress composing her face and manner for the public. Greville Janner, the MP who presented various notables to her, politely remarked that it must be something of a strain meeting so many strangers and shaking so many hands. 'It is not as difficult as it might seem', remarked Her Majesty, deadpan. 'You see I don't have to introduce myself, they all seem to know who I am.'

After an hour the Queen was presented with a seven-branch candelabrum, the menorah used in the Jewish Festival of Lights, and her working week in public was at an end.

No doubt with a sigh of relief she drove off to Sandringham to spend Thursday and Friday in gumboots and husky jacket attending one of her favourite events, the field trials of the Retriever Championships organized by the International Gundog League. She loves dogs and breeds Labradors. The only disappointment was that her own yellow Labrador, Sandringham Salt, was not on top form and did not perform well in the championship.

To make up for that, there was still the weekend to look forward to – a quiet family affair with the Queen, Prince Philip and Prince Andrew staying as guests of Lord and Lady Brabourne at their Kent home, Newhouse. Lady Brabourne is an old friend: the daughter of Earl Mountbatten, she was once leader of the Woodpecker Patrol of the Buckingham Palace Girl Guides, in which the Queen served as a child. There, in the privacy of a family circle, which the Queen so much enjoys, she could really relax right away from the eternal handshaking.

Ronald Payne

Above: The Queen with some of the 'guns' who took part in the retriever trials. She hosted this event at Sandringham and it gave her two enjoyable days out of the public eye. This photograph was taken at Wolverton, which lies to the north-east of the estate, and shows on the left, her agent for the Sandringham estate, Julian Loyd and, on the far right, Sir Joshua Rowley and Lord Somerleyton.

The Queen is a keen dog-breeder herself and royal Labrador puppies are much sought after in the canine world. Naturally, she's the one person in the country who doesn't have to have a dog licence.

The Royal Mews

Lieutenant-Colonel Sir John Miller (right) is the Crown Equerry in charge of the Royal Mews at Buckingham Palace. The many and various vehicles in his care range from the antique Glass Coach (shown behind him) to the pollution-free electric van (below) which Prince Philip uses for short journeys in town. The most important cars in the Mews are the five State Rolls Royces. Mrs John Buckley (centre) is shown here sweeping out the 'Jubilee Rolls', a £100,000 Phantom VI which was given to the Queen in 1978. It has a transparent rear roof, an elevating rear seat ('like a cinema organ's') and detachable bumpers so that it can fit on board the Royal Yacht *Britannia*. A cocktail cabinet was offered and declined, but a stereo tape deck (top right) was installed and equipped with the Queen's favourite military band music.

The Jubilee Rolls is the newest of the State cars: the others are a 1950 Phantom Rolls; a 1954 Phantom IV landaulette which she bought herself second-hand; and then the two 'bubble cars', both Phantom VS with perspex roofs dating from 1960 and 1961. All the State Rollses are painted in 'royal claret', a shade of maroon so dark that it looks almost black, and are devoid of numberplates. They all carry a shield with the royal coat of arms and an optional blue light for use at night. Traffic lights magically turn to green at their approach. Other cars in the Royal Mews include two aged Austin Princesses, and a selection of Ford Escorts, Granadas and Rovers for everyday use. These all have number plates, as do the Royal Family's personal cars – the Queen's dark green 3.5 Rover; Prince Philip's Range Rover; Prince Charles's blue DB6 Aston Martin; and Princess Diana's Ford Escort. The only form of transport which never seems to have found Royal favour is the bicycle – the Queen was given one for her Jubilee but swiftly donated it to charity.

The grandest vehicles in the Royal Mews are the ceremonial coaches: the Speaker's Coach, which is the oldest; the George III State Coach used for coronations; the Irish State Coach used for the opening of Parliament; and the comparatively recent Glass Coach which was bought for King George V's coronation in 1911. King George VI sold seven coaches from the Royal Mews to Alexander Korda for use in films; they had to be borrowed back for the Queen's coronation in 1953. The Mews Stables (right) house thirty horses - the bays, which are used for minor duties, and the famous Windsor Grays which always pull the Queen's carriage. They are trained by being played loud tape recordings of crowd and traffic noises.

This solid silver mascot (below) of Saint George and the Dragon is always transferred to whichever of the State cars the Queen is travelling in. It was designed for her by Edward Seago before her Accession, and was originally executed in sugar as the centrepiece of her wedding cake. The silver 'Kermit' frog (right) was given to Princess Diana by Prince Charles – her 'Frog Prince' – as a twenty-first birthday present. The gundog mascot (below right) belongs to the Queen's Land Rover, and the polo player (next down) is affixed to Prince Charles's Ford Granada.

A family gathering of Royal Rollses at Ascot (left). All the cars without numberplates come from the Royal Mews; the one the Queen is travelling in is the one with St George mascot and watchful chauffeur in attendance. The car with numberplate next to it is the Queen Mother's. Notice the general antiquity of the royal cars – all the State Rollses except one are at least twenty years old, and the Queen has said that she plans to drive her personal car, a 1974 Rover, until it drops. The first ever Royal car was a Daimler, bought by Edward VII as Prince of Wales in 1900. The Royal Family stayed loyal to Daimlers until after the War, when King George VI decided they were too low-built for monarchical dignity and switched to Rolls Royces.

PRINCE PHILIP

Sunday

Fly to Münster/Greven. (After private stay with relatives in Germany.) Buffet supper with Duke of Edinburgh's Royal Regiment 1st Battalion Osnabrück.

Monday

Day with Royal Regiment and REME. Drive to Münchengladbach.

Tuesday

Visit Intelligence Corps, and BAOR RAF Brüggen. Diplomatic Corps reception, Buckingham Palace.

Wednesday

National Playing Fields Assoc. presentations Buckingham Palace. Royal College of Defence Studies. Falklands Campaign Medals ceremony, Buckingham Palace. Reception for British Jews, St James's Palace. CCPR Dinner, Hyde Park Hotel.

Thursday

Trustees meeting, National Maritime Museum. English Speaking Union prize giving, Buckingham Palace. Reception for Friends of Duke of Edinburgh's Award scheme. Ritz Club charity dinner.

Friday

BSG Britax factory, Chichester. Inspect flight simulator, Rediffusion, Crawley. To Lord Brabourne for weekend.

It was just after midday on Monday, and Prince Philip was already posing for his second official group photograph of the week. The atmosphere inside the Officers' Mess of the Duke of Edinburgh's Royal Regiment in Osnabrück was tense. Burgermeister Moller adjusted his silver chain of office. The door opened and Prince Philip entered, escorted by half a dozen officers. He was introduced to the local officials and then an immaculate white-coated waiter entered bearing three glasses of gin and tonic. Prince Philip gestured towards the Burgermeister.

'Gin and tonic?' he asked. 'It looks like all you're going to get.'

'Oh, no, sir, there is anything you want,' said an officer in the obsequious tones bordering on panic which follow the Duke wherever he goes.

For a few moments, there was desultory conversation in German – and then an embarrassed silence. Finally, an officer tried a conversational gambit. 'The mayor has just been to Egypt, sir,' he said hopefully.

'Oh.'

'We are twinned with Derby,' said the Burgermeister, beaming.

'Oh,' repeated Prince Philip. But the conversation could not get airborne and officers gazed at their boots in a way which suggested they were praying for inspiration.

'How much longer do we have to stay here?' asked Prince Philip.

'Only another five minutes, sir,' said an officer.

For thirty-one years, Prince Philip has spent much of his time in situations where even the small talk is fraught. Yet, during a week in which, among other things, he drank at Buckingham Palace with a Russian spy, and simulated flying a Boeing 767 from New York to Kansas City, he did not once publicly betray anything other than professional aptitude for a job which must occasionally have seemed worth far more than the £171,000 annual salary he receives.

His week began at 7.10 on a cold and foggy Sunday evening when he piloted an Andover of the Queen's Flight into Münster/Greven Airport after a four-day private visit to relatives in Germany. As Colonel-in-Chief, he tries to visit the regiment once a year. He changed into black tie at the CO's home for a buffet supper with about fifty officers and wives. 'We treat him as one of us,' said the Adjutant, Captain John Silvester. The remark was to be repeated with varying degrees of sincerity throughout the week.

Next morning, at exactly 9 am, and dressed in a heavy wool jersey and barrack dress trousers, the Duke arrived at battalion headquarters for a briefing about training, followed by a tour of the camp. This was choreographed with all the Army's meticulous efficiency. Squaddies who were a bit lax in sweeping away dirt which might have fouled the ducal shoe, were shooed out of sight. 'He's not in a particularly good mood today, so not too much "up the nose" stuff,' advised one of the Duke's party, which included six regimental officers, two detectives and an equerry.

He had, apparently, been perturbed by

excessively garish methods of protection –
his Daimler was equipped with gas masks
and, outside the Army base, he was accompanied by what he considered to be an
over-enthusiastic convoy of police cars –
though it would have been impossible to
tell from his outward appearance that anything was amiss.

There was judo, a rifle range, a gym and
a kitchen to visit; an inter-platoon competition to watch, and pewter tankards to
be presented to the teams; a group photograph to be taken with the warrant officers
and sergeants; and a wives' club at which
to take tea. It was far less informal than the
rehearsal three days earlier.

'What goes on here, then?' he asked as
he entered a gym – apparently consumed
with interest in the reply. For a few
seconds, every answer had his undivided
attention, in a way that was so intense it
had to be a special technique. 'He does his
homework for each occasion,' said a man
he met later in the week. 'If he sees you out
of context, though, he may not remember
who you are or what your organization is
– even if you run one of his favourite
charities.'

It is fascinating to watch him playing the
crowds. At the wives' club he arrived 20
minutes early, having completed his schedule too soon, and there was embarrassment
about how to fill the time. 'They'd better
do some tap dancing,' muttered an officer.
But Prince Philip, who at first forgot to
remove his cap (thus disconcerting the at-
tendant officers who could not remove
theirs until he had done so), simply made
up time by going twice round the groups
of seated wives and children. His conversational gambits usually ended with a question, so as to provoke a response even from
the tongue-tied. 'You need warm clothing.
It's chilly here, isn't it?' or, to a group of
mothers, 'How many children do you have
between you?'

'Oh, my God, he's got on to the popu-
lation question,' said a worried aide. Only
a few weeks previously he had outraged
some public opinion by telling the Solomon
Islanders that they had too many children
– a gaffe caused when he was taken mistak-
enly into a maternity ward instead of a
geriatric one. He tends to blurt out

To start an inter-platoon competition, Prince Philip strikes the Vernon Bell (main picture), an intriguing naval presence within the khaki confines of a British Army of the Rhine base. When the Duke of Edinburgh's Royal Regiment was established in the late 1950s, Prince Philip urged that they should retain links with the Navy. A close association was formed with HMS Vernon, hence the ship's bell to be found at Osnabrück. Not only that, but the regiment even works to 'ship's time' – the sounding of the bell marks the passing of each four-hour 'watch', ending as it does on a ship, with eight bells. The winning team receives pewter tankards (top left) from the practised royal hand that usually spends much of a business day presenting awards of one kind or another – including raffle prizes at the Wives' Club (left).

Luxury travel is also a perk of royal life although security measures illustrate the ever-present dangers. In Germany, the official car (below) was equipped with gas masks in case of terrorist attack.

thoughts, which might be better left un-
said, when the unexpected happens.

He drew tickets for a raffle from a plastic
shopping bag – 'one way of passing the
time', said an officer – and congratulated
each winner with a warm smile and a 'Well
done'. He must receive an odd impression
of the human species. Most of those he
meets are well dressed, laugh at whatever
he says, and generally make fairly fatuous
replies. His occasional querulous outbursts
are caused by his irritation at continual
sycophancy.

Next, the Officers' Mess, lunch and a
quick change into REME insignia – he is
Colonel-in-Chief of numerous regiments –
for a visit to their factories. White lines had
been freshly painted on the floor, so that
his shoes stuck gently to them. After that it
was a three-hour drive to Münchengladbach
– it was too foggy to travel by Andover, as
planned – and similar visits the following
day to the Intelligence Corps of the British
Army on the Rhine and the Royal Air Force
at Brüggen. He met the relevant local dignitaries, took cocktails with the officers
and their wives, changed from Army uniform to RAF 'woolly pully' (it is no wonder
he needs two full-time valets, one of
whom always travels with him), chatted to
schoolchildren who had been waiting in
the freezing weather to greet him. Then he
piloted himself back to Northolt – Heath-
row was closed because of fog – and Buckingham Palace, for a quick change into
white tie for that evening's Diplomatic
Corps reception, where among the 2,000
guests was Captain Anatoli Zotov, the
Russian naval attaché who was to be ex-
pelled from Britain the next day.

Wednesday was another busy day, starting at 10 am with a short ceremony at
which he presented parchment certificates
to twelve outstanding members of the National Playing Fields Association – he has
been president for thirty-four years – posed
for the inevitable group photograph, visited the Royal College of Defence Studies
with the Queen, presented South Atlantic
Campaign Medals to the Household Division, and then went with the Queen to a
reception given by the Board of Deputies
of British Jews. There the stock question,
'Where do you come from?' produced the

Another uniform – Prince Philip changed into REME insignia in the Ladies' room of the Officers' Mess at Osnabrück before visiting REME factories – and another set of home-made cakes which he decided to pass round himself, much to the evident delight of the assembled wives (top left). 'Are you on a diet?' is always a good conversational ploy. But he is perhaps more at home discussing aspects of the Tornado (bottom left), the latest addition to British defences at RAF Brüggen, which he visited the next day. An avid pilot, he flew himself back from Brüggen in time for a reception for the Diplomatic Corps at Buckingham Palace that evening, but not before charming and delighting a group of British children (right) whose parents work at the base. The flags were handed out in advance to ensure a warm welcome which, in the event, was rapturous and needed no prompting.

Prince Philip pins a South Atlantic Campaign Medal on one of the 942 soldiers of the Household Division who mustered on the lawns of Buckingham Palace on the day after he returned from his flying visit to military bases in Germany. It was one of those rare occasions when three senior members of the family – Philip, Prince Charles, and the Duke of Kent – were present at the same event. There were smiles of pride and satisfaction at moments in an otherwise rather sombre occasion. There was, too, deep concern for the injured. Prince Charles in particular was moved by the suffering he saw and had to be hurried along by his father.

answer, 'Dialystok', from a Polish rabbi. 'Dialystok,' exulted Prince Philip, and then continued in German, 'I know it well.' It is a remote Polish village where he had been hunting as a boy and he chatted animatedly to the surprised rabbi for quite a while. It was noticeable during the week how, when he plunged into groups, he would pick first on the person with the most easily identifiable occupation – such as a parson – using this as a conversation opener.

When stuck for something to say, he uses the age-old seducer's question, 'Haven't we met somewhere before?' He tells the story against himself of the occasion on which he tried this with an anonymous group of Canadian businessmen. The man to whom he spoke looked genuinely alarmed and replied with all seriousness, 'No, but your face looks familiar.'

Then it was off to the Hyde Park Hotel for a working dinner with twenty members of the Central Council of Physical Recreation – he is president of that, too – to discuss sponsorship for minor sports. He stayed an hour longer than expected – until 11.50 pm – and suggested approaching small firms to put money into a 'pot' which

Some of the diversity of Prince Philip's interests was shown on Thursday. He began the day by popping down to Greenwich in his Lucas electric car for a 10.30 am meeting at the National Maritime Museum of which he has been an enthusiastic and knowledgeable Trustee since 1946. While there, he presented the British Empire Medal to retiring head porter George Balls (above). There were three further engagements – a prizegiving for the English Speaking Union, a Duke of Edinburgh Award Scheme reception at the Palace and a charity dinner at the Ritz – to come. The evening before he had been to a working dinner at the Hyde Park Hotel (right) with twenty members of the Council of Physical Recreation to discuss sponsorship for minority interest sports, staying an hour longer than expected.

could then be distributed under the aegis of the CCPR. 'He is one of the most remarkable men in British sport, because of his enormous intelligence and grasp of the subject,' says General Secretary Peter Lawson.

Not the least of Prince Philip's contributions is his ability to act as a catalyst between so many sections of British society, goading those he thinks inefficient, bringing together unlikely people to support causes of which he approves, although sometimes his enthusiasms can prove an expensive luxury for the organization on which he foists them. He read in a newspaper one day about a computer which could translate Chinese characters into English, and persuaded the English Speaking Union to back the inventor. They lost £17,000 on the project.

The secretary of another organization with which he is involved said plaintively, 'It is a pity he sits next to so many cranky people late at night at the dinners he attends, who can inspire him to support some hare-brained schemes.'

Thursday began with a meeting at the National Maritime Museum, of which he is an active trustee, and continued with the

presentation of English Language competition prizes which, as President, he had helped select for the English Speaking Union. ('He has strongly held individual views about the English language, of which we take note,' says the Director-General Alan Lee Williams, cryptically.) A reception followed at Buckingham Palace for Friends of the Duke of Edinburgh's awards. These are people who contribute time, money or facilities to what is perhaps his favourite interest. Arthur Scargill was invited as a courtesy because his predecessor, Joe Gormley, had been a keen supporter of the scheme, but he did not attend – probably just as well because Prince Philip was in one of his more reactionary moods.

He gave vent to his views on the problems of modern education. Clutching first at his left temple he said that the left side of the brain was being developed 'by all

A study in anticipation. The Duke of Edinburgh is about to arrive at a dinner at the Ritz Club in aid of both his award scheme and the Bowls Outdoor Pursuit Centre – an organization which was in some difficulty until his interest was aroused. Whatever the nervousness that preceded his arrival, the forty-four wealthy guests at the dinner pledged £40,000 to the two charities by the time the evening was over.

these sociologists and people who believe in freedom, whereas' – and he now pointed firmly to his right temple – 'the right side which believes in responsibility and building on the past is being neglected'.

He was very much at home in the convivial, all-male gathering which followed – a dinner for forty-four wealthy guests at the Ritz Club in aid of the award scheme and the Bowls Outdoor Pursuit Centre in Tunbridge Wells, which was on the verge of bankruptcy until Prince Philip intervened several years ago.

The guests, ranging from Eric Morecambe to a wealthy Saudi Arabian businessman, contributed £40,000 to the charities. Prince Philip left at midnight, another late night. But at least, with the Queen away at Sandringham, he would not have to listen to the gallant Pipe Major Brian Macrae in the morning.

Friday was the only day in this particular week to provide anything remotely like 'controversy'. He arrived 23 minutes late for a visit to see car safety equipment at the Britax factory in Chichester and as he drew up to the gates in the Range Rover (OXR 1) he uses for engagements outside London (in town he drives around in a green Lucas electric van) it appeared he was not wearing a safety belt. In fact, he had slipped it off seconds before arriving but it became a main item on the local radio news, and television reporters went up at separate times to ask if he always wore seat belts. 'Yes,' he snapped to one. But the other received the classic ducal brush-off – a withering stare, total silence and complete disregard of his presence.

Prince Philip, a man of mercurial moods, can switch in an instant from affability to cold irascibility, from being one of the boys to reminding the other boys just who he is.

He is not amused by jocular references to his background and finds one nickname – 'Phil the Greek' – deeply offensive. Asked once by a Daughter of the American Revolution to 'tell us about your German ancestry', the man christened Philippos Schleswig-Holstein-Sonderburg-Glücksburg replied haughtily, 'I am Danish.'

And so, after being presented with a collage made of bits and pieces from the Britax factory – 'What a remarkable construc-

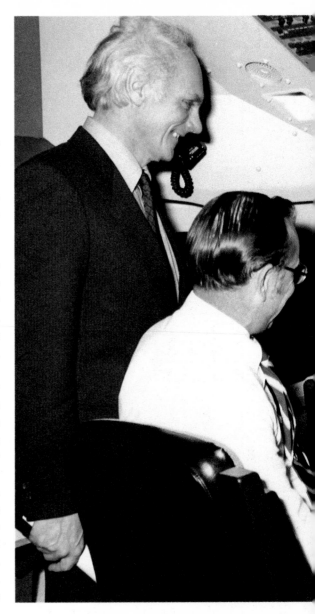

tion,' he said tactfully – he lunched at a local restaurant and then drove through beautiful countryside for a visit to the aircraft simulator in Crawley.

No week of Prince Philip's is 'typical', but this had been as hard-working as most. He had not given one of the eighty or so major speeches he makes each year, nor had he been presented with any new honours (what *do* you give a man who is already Grand Cordon of The Supreme Order of the Chrysanthemum?) but he had put on a bravura performance, faultless in its execution and enthusiastic in its reception. As one person who entertained him observed, 'He is a marvellous public relations man – because he believes in the product he is selling.'

Andrew Duncan

In his element again
(above), Prince Philip
prepares for a flight from
New York to Kansas City
to round off his week. This
was Friday afternoon and
actually he never got
further than a Crawley,
Sussex, industrial complex.
The Boeing 767 cockpit
was a flight simulator and
the 'flight' apparently went
without hitch. Before
lunch he had been at a seat
belt factory in Chichester
where he charmed an
informal overalled guard
of honour (right) who
wore Prince Philip lapel
badges.

The Queen's Flight

Set up (as the King's Flight) by Edward VIII in 1936, the Queen's Flight now consists of three 20-year-old turbo-prop Andovers, two Westland Wessex helicopters and one Bassett communications aircraft. Based at RAF Benson in Oxfordshire, and staffed by 140 RAF volunteers, it makes some sixty flights a month. Long keen to modernize its equipment, Prince Philip has test-piloted a British Aerospace 146–100 jet, two of which are being evaluated by the RAF as replacements for the Andovers.

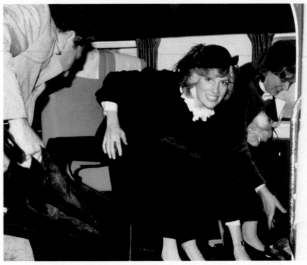

During trips in British airspace by the Andovers of the Queen's Flight, 'Purple Air Space' comes into operation. Like an invisible red carpet in the sky, air traffic routes are cleared and declared 'purple air space': on the ground, all military exercises cease for 45 minutes each side of the time the royal aircraft passes overhead.

The Princess of Wales has become the latest member of the Royal Family to make frequent use of the Queen's Flight. It took her, for instance, to Monaco (left) for the funeral of Princess Grace in 1982. And her husband of course piloted his bride to Gibraltar at the start of their honeymoon in 1981 – despite the fact that the journey took nine hours (including a refuelling stop) in the antiquated Andover, compared with a mere three on a scheduled commercial flight. Among other frequent users of the Flight are the many and various royal pets: Princess Anne (right) watches one of her gundogs enjoy the regal treatment normally reserved for her mother's corgis. If the Royal Family enjoy airborne privileges unknown to its subjects, they do share one common fate aloft: British Airways food, reheated in the Andover's galley.

Prince Charles and Prince Philip are the most frequent users of the Queen's Flight, often piloting themselves to see who can clock up more flying hours each year. The Prince of Wales learnt to fly in the twin-engined Bassett communications aircraft which still belongs to the Flight, and subsequently became a skilled helicopter pilot during his service in the Fleet Air Arm. The monarch never flies by helicopter, as a matter of Palace safety policy, except on the rare occasions when security considerations make it unavoidable (as on her visit to Northern Ireland in 1977). Helicopters are, however, the favourite mode of transport of the Queen Mother, and once, after a forced landing, she happily continued her journey in a relief chopper.

The distinctive red-and-blue markings common to all aircraft of the Queen's Flight make a dramatic sight at airports all over the world: on arrival the captain proudly fixes the Royal Standard aloft, through a slot in the roof of the cockpit, as he taxis towards the welcoming committee.

THE PRINCE OF WALES

Royalist fervour greets Prince Charles on a morale-boosting mission to the depressed town of Consett, County Durham.

The sniffer dogs had left and there was a long buzz of static on a walkie-talkie. Two men, dressed in dark formal suits, were standing at the door, the one tense and clearly sweating. A beefy plain-clothes policeman crossed the foyer and unbuttoned his jacket with a flick of his fingers as he turned to face the small waiting crowd.

Outside the building the streets of London were grey and dripping with mists. There was a distant shout as a black Ford Granada estate, WYN 1 S, pulled up outside the door and a small man with brown terrier-like eyes leaped out.

It was 10.15 am outside the Royal Arts Society in John Adam Street and, punctual as usual, H R H The Prince of Wales, Prince Charles, K G, K T, G C B, had arrived for the first appointment of his working week with the Royal Forestry Society.

As he stepped out of the car accompanied by Francis Cornish, his assistant private secretary, the Prince's most striking feature was his smile, which, somehow and despite all the odds, stayed there. His cheeks were ruddy with the rude good health that comes from regular outdoor exercise, with a tiny scar atop his right cheekbone. His hair was longer than usual and cunningly combed at the rear to cover his bald spot. He was wearing a light grey suit with black shoes and, fittingly, a Royal Forester's badge and tie.

As he was greeted by Sir Marcus Welby the Prince's body rocked back slightly while his eyebrows shot up, as though enjoying some improbable joke. There is little lustre in his eyes but though they are al-

ways seeking other eye contact they will often drop down to study a person's tie, or even feet. He immediately began talking to everyone he was introduced to with a line of chatter which was remarkable. Prince Charles can talk to anyone about almost anything. No one is allowed to initiate a conversation with him – or change the subject once it has begun – but, within half an hour, his subjects had swung from coconut trees to oak trees to police cars without lights to the heath fritillary butterfly.

Upstairs, in the chandeliered conference room, the air was as warm and stuffy as the inside of a bread-bin and there was a rising buzz of excitement as some hundred foresters waited for the Prince to deliver his address. H R H is Colonel-in-Chief of more than fifteen regiments, patron of umpteen societies and member of just about everything, but this morning he belonged to the foresters: sturdy, ruddy men, for the most part, with big strong hands.

The Prince delivered his speech on the forest as an eco-system with all the calm authority of a salesman whose goods enjoy such high quality they hardly need talking about. His style of public speaking is markedly different to his private manner. In conversation he can have an almost drowsy languor, but now he was stiffer with his hands moving up and down the length of his body, now clasping together as if in prayer, now going into his pockets or tugging the bottom of his jacket. Sometimes he scraped the side of his nose with a forefinger. His voice changed too, doing his famous imitation of Mike Yarwood as

49

Prince Charles taking a hedge in style during his day out with the Quorn. Despite her alleged dislike of the sport, Princess Diana followed the hunt in a Range Rover. Hunting is one of Prince Charles's main enthusiasms, though perhaps the least publicized. His country home, Highgrove, lies in the heart of Beaufort country and he usually manages to hunt with them or the Quorn once a week. But he never attends the meet, preferring to join the hunt after it has moved off, to avoid undue attention.

he stretched back his lips a lot to attack the consonants.

As he spoke, his private secretary, sitting in the front row, exchanged notes with his private detective sitting behind him. These two men play an important role in the Prince's public life, fulfilling his almost every need from shooing away intrusive Press photographers to lending the Prince money which, on several occasions now, he has forgotten to pay back.

He attends over two hundred public engagements a year, ranging from opening buildings to diving down to see the Mary Rose. This week provided some sharp contrasts and none more so than the next engagement when, after a light buffet lunch with the foresters, he drove to old Billings-

gate Market to see an archaeological dig.

Sea mists hung over the swollen river while, down a huge hole, clouds of evil black smoke were belching out of a yellow generator and about fifty people were down on their knees clawing the ground frantically like dogs who had lost their favourite bones. 'Just goes to show what a royal visit can do,' a policeman said knowingly. 'Normally there's about six scratching away down there and I can't think where they got this lot from. Must 'ave brought 'em in from the pyramids.'

They were excavating the 12th-century waterfront and old church of St Botolph and, once out of his car at 3 pm, the Prince had quickly changed into Wellington boots and safety helmet before being taken down

into the hole with its dark, incomprehensible tangle of beams and old moorings.

Here the Prince was as clearly happy as a kid making sand castles: while all the officials above stood around the hole jumping up and down to keep warm, he sloshed through the mud for over an hour asking question after question. 'I must say I was very surprised indeed by the penetration of his questions and what he already knew about our dig,' said Brian Hobley, his escort. The Prince was, after all, once an archaeology student at Cambridge.

The next day the Prince, together with the Duke of Edinburgh and the Duke of Kent, was due to pin campaign medals on 942 Falklands veterans on the lawns of Buckingham Palace. It was a day of wintry savagery; a hard cold wind swept around the Palace, and every footstep produced a squelch. To one side were nineteen guardsmen in wheelchairs who were badly wounded in the campaign; with their long plumes of breath vaporizing in the cold, they looked more like members of a routed army than a victorious one.

The Prince himself, dressed in his uniform of Colonel-in-Chief of the Welsh Guards, seemed slightly restless and fidgety as the medals were handed out. He was certainly the most affected by the sight of the wounded in wheelchairs and he proceeded slowly down the line – so slowly indeed that he had spoken to only four or five before he was summoned back to join the Duke of Edinburgh and the Duke of

Kent on the saluting base for the march past.

The pipes skirled, the drums drummed, the brass bands declaimed the old tunes of glory – 'Scotland the Brave', 'Sospan Fach', 'God Bless the Prince of Wales.' Such things unleash the emotions and Prince Charles stood to attention struggling with them. As the parade finally disappeared into the afternoon mist, he hesitated a moment, then addressed his father, right arm raised and fluttering like a schoolboy's. 'I won't be long,' he murmured, 'I'm just going . . .'

With that he walked briskly down the steps towards the line of wounded, clearly determined to speak to them all before leaving. There was a slight flutter, for the move was unexpected, and an aide ran forward to clear the way. A girl from one of the soldiers' families rushed forward with her instant camera. Prince Charles smiled and half halted, then pressed on to the serious business of the afternoon. He returned to the point in the wheelchair line where he had left off and could be heard engaging each of the wounded guardsmen in conversation. He stopped in front of one Welsh guardsman, Simon Weston, whose head was shaven, eyes sunk deep in misshapen sockets, the side of his face a raw tangle of healing burns. 'You get well soon,' the Prince said. The guardsman replied, 'Yes sir. I will.'

Next day the Prince had a private engagement – an informal lunch with the Law Society at their headquarters in Chancery Lane. There at 12.30 pm he was met at the door by John Bowran, the General Secretary, and Max Williams, the president. He was then escorted into the main hall, where again the Prince spoke to everyone present – all sixty-five members of the council and eight senior employees – about everything from ties to sailing, the *Mary Rose*, Billingsgate Market, advocacy, computers and word-processors. He always made the conversational running and at one point actually complained that when a subject got really interesting he had to move on.

After the morning speech to the Royal Forestry Society, praising the virtues of 'the forest as ecosystem' (top left), Prince Charles dons wellingtons and safety helmet to inspect an archaeological dig beside the Thames at Billingsgate Market (above and right). Museum of London organizers showed him the Roman and Saxon quaysides they had unearthed, and the Prince chatted knowledgeably about jointing techniques.

Prince Charles talks to soldiers wounded in the Falklands Campaign. After presenting South Atlantic Medals and taking the salute with his father and the Duke of Kent (right), Prince Charles returned to talk again to the wounded, anxious not to miss any one out.

The council members – a suspicious, crusty bunch for the most part – were very impressed. 'It was a brilliant performance and it does take a lot to impress us,' said John Bowran.

Over a light lunch the Prince took a glass of water which is typical of his ascetic life-style. He always rises at 6.30 am, never takes alcohol during the day and is virulently anti-smoking to the point of choking apoplexy if he sees someone light up. He has a tax-free income of some £580,000 a year but never carries money around with him. His dress is unrepentantly traditional and he is a self-avowed and proud square.

His deep compassion is revealed again and again in the course of his public engagements – his sympathy for those in wheel chairs, his patience with the mentally handicapped, the way he comes to the crowds – and they to him.

That night he attended the première of a film about the most holy ascetic of them all, Mahatma Gandhi. In contrast to the

mud of Billingsgate and the dankness of the Palace lawns this was a glittering occasion – a sudden glimpse of the lush and laundered life – as beautiful stars with their beautiful paste jewels and beautifully capped teeth milled around the royal enclosure inside the cinema greeting one another. The younger stars looked petrified, while the older stars – possibly fortified beforehand by a few large drinks – went around smacking huge theatrical kisses on one another's cheeks.

And then came an opening in a huge bank of bodies and in walked the Prince, followed by the stunning Princess Diana who still meets the public by peering out of the corner of her eyes.

The Prince was his usual picture of sunny and affable charm, commiserating with Sir Richard Attenborough, the film's director. 'What a relief it must be to get it all off your chest. You were in New Delhi yesterday weren't you? And in New York tomorrow. God. Living out of a suitcase is no fun.'

Next morning the contrast was vivid. After the première the Prince had taken the Royal Train out of King's Cross station and travelled overnight to Consett, County Durham, where at 9.30 am he stepped down some makeshift wooden stairs in to a muddy railway siding next to vast piles of gleaming black coal.

Prince Charles arrives for an informal lunch at the Law Society, with its President, Max Williams. The Prince met all sixty-five members of the council and talked about everything from word processors to sailing.

The Royal Train

The night before, he had attended a film première in London. The morning after, the Prince of Wales was due bright and early in Consett, County Durham. The answer to such logistical problems is a good night's sleep aboard the Royal Train, which pulls into Consett (right) after allowing HRH a few peaceful hours in a nearby siding. Amid strict security, the Prince disembarks just outside town (below), and transfers to a royal limo. The train is rarely seen pulling into BR stations, again for security reasons, and when not in use is tucked away in sidings at Wolverton, in Buckinghamshire. Apart from his parents, Prince Charles is perhaps the most frequent user of the Royal Train, often using its extensive facilities to write speeches and catch up with paperwork on his way to and from public engagements. Once the Royal Family paid for the ride: today all Royal Train journeys are classified state business, and financed by the government.

The Queen's apartments in the present Royal Train – which came into service in 1977, her Silver Jubilee year – were furnished by Sir Hugh Casson. The pale blue velvet cushions are hand-stitched; the paintings on the wall are of previous, rather more splendid, Royal Trains. Prince Philip's apartments (far right) are a more masculine shade of brown, and include a kitchen and dining room capable of serving meals for up to ten people. A familiar sight when the claret-coloured coaches reach their destination is the arrival of a makeshift platform to ease Royal disembarkation.

Consett is set in the unemployed heart-land of the North-East, and the town's poverty seems to seep out of the streets. Most of all this poverty is proclaimed by the crumbling edifice of the steel works – once Consett's famous centre – now look-ing as if a nuclear missile has hit it since it is being torn down and sold for scrap. Here one in three men is out of work and, on some estates, two in three.

Yet no sooner had Prince Charles come up the railway bank than he was greeted by a rolling roar of unconfined ecstasy which went rolling on all day: mile after unwinding mile of handshakes, pats on babies' heads, Union-Jack-waving tod-dlers, overwhelmed grannies, cheering mothers and even punks, including one harpy with a safety pin in her ear, a studded bondage jacket and torn stockings.

At his first stop on the new industrial estate the Prince went over to a gang of skinheads standing behind a barbed wire fence. 'What are you yobbos doing behind that fence?' the Prince asked. There was a

After escorting Princess Diana to the première of *Gandhi* (top), Prince Charles took the Royal Train overnight to Consett, County Durham. He emerged at the muddy rundown sidings of Old Consett station after breakfast to be greeted by a thousand-strong crowd, including protesters from the Derwentside Rail Action Group who want to reopen the Consett to Newcastle railway line.

Everywhere he went in Consett, the Prince was greeted by enthusiastic crowds, and he stopped and talked to many of them. He told one group of retired steelworkers that he would do all he could to attract new industry to the town, where unemployment runs at thirty per cent. Later he visited the site of the famous old steel works – now being demolished and sold for scrap.

sagging silence as the skinheads' mouths opened and closed wondering if the Prince had really called them yobbos. 'Got a job have you?' the Prince asked again.

'On the dole,' one skinhead said finally whereupon the Prince shook his hand adding that he hoped he would get a job soon. Later in the morning the Prince spotted the skinhead again and yet again shook his hand saying that he hoped things would look up.

To a redundant steelworker he said 'Geordies never give up' – a remark which found its way into all the local newspaper headlines and ended up on billposters within two hours of him making it.

He was also given a tub of truffles on the estate, the first in a series of presents that day which included a packet of toffee, a packet of cheese-flavoured corn curls called – appropriately enough – 'Big Charlie's', a leather book on the history of Northumberland, a squeaky ball for baby William, a Christmas card and a ceramic Welsh dragon wearing a coronet and diving wet suit clutching a model of the *Mary Rose*.

After a buffet lunch at the Town Hall the planned helicopter flight to open the new £9m Northumberland County Hall had to be cancelled because of freezing fog so the Prince had to make the journey by road. All day the fog kept bedevilling the arrangements. 'Remember you've only seen a fraction of what goes on in a week,' the Prince's assistant private secretary, Francis Cornish, said grimly. 'And here we are in Northumberland stuck in the fog and not a clue how we are going to get home. Think about it.'

By 3.30 pm the band outside the County Hall were chattering to their instruments in the purest cold as the Prince walked down to the hall's entrance. All around him there was a hullabaloo of cheers, waves and detectives bundling away photographers who got too close. The Prince spotted a line of wheelchairs and was off in a flash, asking if they came far. About ten feet behind the royal group a man from local radio was gibbering into a microphone while turning round and round in tight demented circles in a way that suggested he was about to be flung into his own padded cell very soon. 'So

'What are you yobbos doing behind that fence?' was HRH's opening sally to this group of out-of-work youngsters in Berry Edge Road, Consett. One of them, eighteen-year-old John McAloon, explained afterwards that he and his mates had just gone to have a look at the Prince, and were very surprised when he talked to them. 'He asked if I had a job and I told him that I was on the dole. Then he shook my hand. I think he is a great man and it has made me more patriotic than ever,' he said.

In opening the new £9m Northumberland County Hall, Prince Charles was finishing off a job begun by his grandmother when she laid the foundation stone more than three years ago. He was greeted by the Pegswood Band (left) and by Robin Birley, his ex-history teacher from Gordonstoun and now the Council Chairman. 'I couldn't resist doing something for him,' said the Prince. 'He managed to ensure that I passed my A levels and got an S level.'

here I am now with Prince Charles and the crowds are cheering wildly ...' Soon he had got so carried away he was actually looking in the opposite direction to the group. 'And there's a lot of children waving flags ...' Back on course again. 'And now he's meeting his old history teacher ...'

Some of the handshakes were more like wrenches in all the excitement and HRH clearly needed all the beefiness he has built up over the years as Royal Action Man – the polo player, fox hunter, wind surfer and deep sea diver.

In a short speech, the Prince declared the building open and, later, while looking around its impressive corridors with their local glass and brickwork, shouted up at some council workers with perhaps the loudest hint of the week. 'I see you've got some tea up there,' he bellowed. 'I'm hoping to get some myself very soon.'

He got his tea very soon and the party was off again, via a new local business centre and on through the dripping darkness to the town of Morpeth where the red carpet had been rolled out at the Town Hall and the Prince climbed a staircase festooned with fresh flowers to be received by the Lord Mayor in his parlour. The Mayor presented him with a leather-bound history of Morpeth.

'Ah some more light bedtime reading,' the Prince cracked before signing the visitors' book and a huge coloured poster of himself. His handwriting is broad and rather unformed – almost childlike.

On leaving the Town Hall at 5.55 pm he was presented with three single carnations by three toddlers before moving off for one of his little walkabouts which give the crowds such joy and his detectives such gloom. The coloured Christmas lights – switched on a week early for his visit – gave the scene a gaudy theatricality as he moved from group to group.

Spasms of emotion went rolling round the crowds in the square while he seemed to create a goosepimpled warmth around him as if he were a bonfire. Even as his Daimler moved off, carrying him away for a free weekend in Gloucestershire, the warmth seemed to stay in the air and brighten the night.

Tom Davies

After touring various exhibitions, the Prince's next task at Morpeth was to open the new Northumberland Business Centre (top). There he was presented with an eight-inch-high red pottery dragon (left) which he accepted with apparent delight. From there he went on to Morpeth Town Hall (above) where he was given yet another unexpected gift, a History of Morpeth. He talked to the Mayor, Councillor Geoff Brown and other officials in the Mayor's Parlour (far left) and signed the visitors' book. Then he went on a walkabout through the town while his aides frantically pondered the problem of how to get home – it was too foggy to use the helicopter.

THE PRINCESS OF WALES

For the *Gandhi* première,
Princess Diana, wears one
of the evening dresses she
bought during her
engagement – a Bellville
Sassoon creation in filmy
silk chiffon. She was
presented with a bouquet
of orchids enclosing an
extremely large gold
brooch.

As far as the world's Press are concerned, all the Royal Family except one could drop off the face of the Earth tomorrow without making much noticeable difference to their front pages. Royal coverage is now concentrated almost exclusively on one person – the Princess of Wales. 'You can't *give* photos of Prince Charles away,' one regular Royal photographer commented gloomily. There are other Royals who are more important, more intelligent, more hardworking, even possibly (Princess Michael of Kent) more beautiful, but there is none who arouses such sustained and passionate public interest.

So by 9.30 am on Tuesday there were the men from the *Sun*, the *Star*, the *Mirror* and all the other royal photographers jostling on their aluminium step-ladders outside a tiny crumbling youth club in Catford, because the Princess of Wales was due to arrive there in an hour's time. They call themselves the Royal Pack; the Palace has been known to call them 'the Scum'; Harry Arnold of the *Sun* protests – 'But we're the *crème de la* Scum.'

The Pack was more than usually straining at the leash on Tuesday because it was the Princess's first public outing for several days. She had spent the weekend quietly at Wood Farm, Sandringham, with Prince Charles and baby Prince William, and Wood Farm is a well-known dead loss for sneak photographers because it can be reached only across a million acres of ploughed fields. (Highgrove, on the other hand, is a doddle for telephoto lenses which may well be the reason Prince

Charles is thinking of selling it.) On Monday Prince Charles went hunting with the Quorn, and Princess Diana followed in a Range Rover driven by Lady King, wife of the Chairman of British Airways. No doubt the Pack would have followed too, if they had known, but of course they didn't till later – the hunting crowd are notoriously discreet.

'She'll be late,' said the photographers, 'she always is. Except when she's with Prince Charles of course.' And sure enough, she was late, though only by about five minutes. A dark green, surprisingly modest Vauxhall estate with plastic seats and dog-gate, suddenly drew into the kerb and there she was. The crowd of housewives and schoolchildren almost missed her because they were staring at the much posher red Rover which drew up behind – but that was only the backup car, containing her detective.

The Princess got out of her car, shook hands with the Mayor of Lewisham, and then paused for a few moments to smile at the crowd and collect two red roses from children. This, the photographers say, is something she has learnt since she became a Royal. In the early Coleherne Court days, she used to put her head down and bomb straight forward to wherever she was heading for, but now she has learnt to stand still for a minute, with her head up and a nice smile and wave, to give them a decent closeup.

She was wearing a bottle green suit with piped shoulders (which she has worn several times before), burgundy handbag and shoes, and nasty pale glitter tights. There

were two powdery blobs on the back of her skirt as though she had sat on some cake crumbs (*breakfast* in the *car?*) and she was surprisingly heavily made up with lavish triangles of blusher and shader on her cheeks. 'Isn't she thin?' the crowd all murmured, inspired by recent press stories of anorexia. Certainly she looked much thinner than at her engagement début in that memorable black lowcut dress, but in fact she shed most of her puppy fat between then and the wedding.

Then the Princess disappeared inside the building for 90 minutes to talk to social workers and Catford youth (mainly black teenage girls). The visit was her own idea, suggested from the Palace about a fortnight beforehand, because the Centre is partly funded by Prince Charles' Jubilee Trust. No journalists were allowed into the building. Most other Royals allow at least a token press presence wherever they go but the Princess doesn't, perhaps because she is

At the Hearsay Youth Aid Centre in Catford, south London, Princess Diana talks to young people about accommodation and employment problems. On arrival, she was handed several single red roses by children in the crowd – this is becoming a regular Princess Diana trademark. Then she spent 90 minutes inside the Centre talking to social workers and teenagers. They had all decided to 'dress normally' for the occasion so jeans and plimsolls were the order of the day, but they did, in deference to the Princess, stop smoking for the duration. It was the Princess's own idea to visit the Centre, which receives an annual £8,000 grant from the Royal Jubilee Trust, a trust set up by Prince Charles in Jubilee Year to encourage youth projects.

Nurses and patients spill
onto the balconies to
welcome Princess Diana to
The Hospital for Sick
Children in Great Ormond
Street. The hospital has
strong Royal connections –
the Queen is its patron,
and Princess Alexandra
did her nursing training
here.

The Princess, in a cerise
suit, looks elated and
confident on arrival. Her
experience at the Young
England kindergarten
stands her in good stead as
she meets play leader
Megan Morris and three-
year-old Jenna Hartley
(centre) in the outpatients'
playroom. Jenna wore a
Union Jack hat for the
occasion and stood on a
chair for a better view.
'You're looking very tall
up there,' said the Princess.

still unsure of herself. Consequently, all the reporters dashed inside as soon as she had gone to ask all the Catford youth what she had said. They said she seemed interested and friendly and well-informed and her handshake was firm.

That afternoon, according to paparazzi, the Princess went shopping in Harvey Nichols, Knightsbridge, as she often does, driving herself in her black Ford Escort with the silver 'Kermit' frog mascot – Prince Charles, her frog prince, gave it to her for her 21st. Rumour has it that she now takes *two* detectives on her shopping expeditions – one to accompany her through the shop and the other to stave off parking wardens. In the evening she went with other Royals to a reception at the Palace for the diplomatic corps.

On Wednesday the Princess stayed at home in Kensington Palace all day, much to the frustration of the photographers waiting outside. No doubt she enjoyed playing with baby William – it is known that she likes bathing him to the strains of Roger Scott on Capital Radio between four and seven. She is a great fan of Capital – Prince Charles prefers Radio 3. She also likes watching *Crossroads* and *Dallas* and reading romantic novels, including those of her stepgrandmother, Barbara Cartland. She probably spent some time on correspondence – next day there was a letter on her car's dashboard addressed in girlish

The Princess talks to the nurses who lined her route between wards. She visited the intensive care unit, two surgical wards and the outpatients' playroom, staying 25 minutes longer than scheduled. The hospital's Governor, Mr Bill Milchen, said afterwards, 'She was absolutely marvellous. The staff and children loved her. She is so very natural and she has a way with children that is truly fantastic.'

handwriting to Broadlands, the home of her friends Lord and Lady Romsey.

Thursday morning's appointment was at Great Ormond Street Children's Hospital where all the balconies were alive with cheering nurses and patients. The Princess looked gorgeous in a cerise suit and smiled with real elation at the crowd. She was accompanied this time by the Queen's assistant press secretary, Victor Chapman, a burly fifty-year-old Canadian, formerly press officer to Pierre Trudeau, as well as by her handsome detective, Graham Smith, who looks like Dr David Owen.

After visiting several wards (freshly spruced up with new paint) she came into the huge outpatients' playroom where about a hundred children and their parents awaited her. She really *is* good with children, indeed brilliant. Unlike many other Royals whose physical repertoire seems to begin and end with the handshake, she is very tactile – she readily pats a baby's head, or plays with its fingers, or squats down or bends over (showing her

Princess Diana arrives at the royal première of *Gandhi* where she meets the stars including actor Ben Kingsley (below) who plays the Mahatma. She was also presented to Sir Richard Attenborough, the film's director, and actors Sir John Gielgud, Sir John Mills, and Trevor Howard. Other celebrities at the première included Terry Wogan, Ringo Starr, and the Princess's stepgrandmother, Barbara Cartland. Prince Charles was particularly keen to see the film because it was dedicated to his muchloved great-uncle, the late Earl Mountbatten of Burma, and proceeds of the première went to the Mountbatten Trust, of which he is Chairman. It was Lord Mountbatten who enlisted the aid of the Indian government in the making of the film.

white slip in the process) to converse at a child's eyelevel, and she asks the sort of questions – 'What's your doll called?' 'Do you like having a big sister?' – which children respond to. One little boy greeted her aggressively with 'I ain't got no flowers for you.' 'Well smell these then,' she said, handing over her bouquet. 'Yukk!' And she giggled with delight. Children bring out the very best in her: amused and relaxed, no longer just a pretty face, she visibly gains in confidence.

By contrast, that evening's engagement, the Royal première of *Gandhi*, showed her back in her purely decorative role. She arrived on time for this one, being with Prince Charles, and she wore a magical white, blue and pink off-the-shoulder Bellville Sassoon dress that she wore once before at the Victoria and Albert Museum. She seemed to have a cold and sounded a bit snuffly. Prince Charles went along the receiving line first, and Princess Diana followed a few paces behind, being separately introduced to all the bigwigs. Her problem was having to dream up new questions that Prince Charles hadn't already asked, and her powers of invention occasionally failed her. 'Did you go to the première in Delhi?' was a favourite effort. 'Are you going to the American première?' was another. She told one bemused producer that it was 'nice to see a *good* film for once, unlike all those dreadful films, *if-you-know-what-I-mean.*'

Then a protocolian disaster struck. Prince Charles was introduced to Sir Richard Attenborough and greeted him as an old friend, then Attenborough broke ranks and followed along the line with the Prince, taking over the introductions himself. This left the Princess standing uncertainly before the hole in the line that should have been Sir Richard Attenborough. Suddenly Sir Richard realized his gaffe, spun round and practically fell over her. While he made elaborate actorish apologies, she did a mock-rueful, 'Oh don't worry about me – I always tag along behind.' But she was definitely a bit thrown.

The next morning the Princess was up early (due at 10, instead of her usual 10.30) to visit the Department of Health and Social Security at Elephant & Castle. The

A picket of Civil and Public Services Association strikers awaits Princess Diana at the headquarters of the Department of Health and Social Security. But good humour prevails as she arrives with her personal detective (centre) and Social Services Secretary Mr Norman Fowler in close attendance. The Princess stayed for two hours being briefed on child welfare benefits. Perhaps she applied for her own child allowance – she is entitled to £5.85 per week. Afterwards, she treated herself and her lady-in-waiting, Miss Anne Beckwith-Smith, to lunch at the *Ménage à Trois* restaurant in Knightsbridge.

Pack, of course, was waiting, together with a crowd of twenty-odd housewives, and a small picket of DHSS strikers. Everyone debated how the Princess would cope with the picket, but in the event it was very simple – the police lined them up on the left and the crowd on the right and the Princess walked straight from her car to the building (12 minutes late) with her eyes firmly right. She was wearing a fawn wrap-over coat and no hat. There were no hats all week – the British millinery industry will crumble back to dust.

After the visit, which lasted two hours, the Princess went off for lunch at the trendy *Ménage à Trois* restaurant in Beauchamp Place, Knightsbridge. Her lady-in-waiting and detective had been there the day before to case the joint and make the booking. The Princess shared a table with her lady-in-waiting, Miss Anne Beckwith-Smith, while her two detectives sat at the next one. She ate *crudités* (raw vegetables) and a mixed fish dish, and left at about 2.15 asking for the bill to be sent to the Palace. Royal visits to restaurants are rare (Princess Margaret is the only regular restaurant-goer) and this was almost certainly Princess Diana's first such excursion since her marriage. Its object may well have been to scotch press stories about anorexia, since she must have known that news of it would leak out. Afterwards she went to Highgrove for the weekend, driving down with Prince Charles and Prince William,

the Queen having waived the rule about heirs to the throne not travelling together.

This was the week in which Nigel Dempster, the *Mail*'s gossip, went on American television to say that Princess Diana was a 'spoilt monster', domineering, obsessive and extravagant. Who knows? On her public appearances she was graceful and charming, far more ready to smile than many Royals, and in a genuinely friendly way. Everyone who met her during the week was clearly enchanted by her and her way of talking to children was a joy to behold. And there cannot be any other twenty-one-year-old in the world who can give so much pleasure to so many people, just with a smile and a wave.

Lynn Barber

The Pack

This is the scene that greets Princess Diana whenever she puts her nose out of doors – dozens, and sometimes hundreds, of photographers from all over the world, waiting to capture her every expression. It all began in the late summer of 1980 when a group of professional Royal-watchers, truffling along the banks of the Dee at Balmoral in hopes of finding Prince Charles fishing with Anna Wallace, found instead Prince Charles fishing with an unknown blonde. The blonde was quickly identified as Lady Diana Spencer, and on 8 September banner headlines announced 'The New Girl for Charles.' This was followed by the 'Siege of Coleherne Court' when, for five months, photographers camped outside Lady Diana's flat.

No sooner was the engagement announced than Lady Diana appeared in That Dress (right) and sent the Press into a frenzy again. Prudence Glynn of *The Times* called her 'a fashion disaster in her own right' and said the dress made her look as if she were sitting in a hip bath. Alastair Burnett on News at Ten seriously debated the question of whether a nipple had been exposed. (It hadn't.) But the brouhaha evidently taught Lady Diana a lesson: she has never worn such a low décolletage in public again. With the engagement, Diana moved into Clarence House and was better protected from the Press than she had been before. Even so, she burst into tears and fled from a polo match just five days before the wedding, clearly overwhelmed.

Press vigil (left) outside St Mary's, Paddington, with everyone waiting for news of Princess Diana's baby. The mood on that occasion was friendly – Prince Charles came out after the birth to share his joy with photographers and to ask them to keep quiet (which they did) so that the Princess could get a good night's sleep. But relations turned sour again in late 1982 when the Press started running stories about Princess Diana being anorexic, and the Queen had to intervene to ask Editors to lay off. Press-Palace hostilities flared again in January 1983 when cameramen invaded a private ski-ing holiday in Liechtenstein. The Princess resorted to her old Coleherne Court habit of hiding her face from the cameras and Prince Charles had to beg her, 'Please, Diana, be reasonable.'

PRINCESS ANNE

Princess Anne and Mark
Phillips riding out with the
Beaufort hunt, which
meets conveniently near
Gatcombe Park. She hunts
less than he does, and
conflicting engagements
mean they rarely hunt
together. They both
remain avid three-day
eventers and Princess Anne
exercises her horses daily,
getting up especially early
to fit in with official duties.
In keeping with royal
tradition, she has taught
her son Peter to ride and
he was given his first pony
at an early age.

'You don't have to be crazy about children to want to give them a better start in life,' said Princess Anne, explaining her support for the Save the Children Fund. The Fund is one of the Princess' favourite charities and never has she proved her support more convincingly than during three weeks in October/November 1982.

On a gruelling, whirlwind trip she toured seven African and north African countries from Swaziland to Beirut, visiting clinics, villages, refugee camps and attending official receptions. The day often began at 6.30 am and ended at 11 pm. Her stamina and enthusiasm impressed everyone who travelled with her – including the previously lukewarm Press. The Princess travelled with a lady-in-waiting and a security man wherever she went but she had only one other assistant to help with her clothes and she looked after her long hair herself. A member of staff remembers one particularly bumpy plane ride when Princess Anne was trying to change outfits with difficulty. 'She poked her head round the door to us, laughing, and said "Who's driving this thing? Shouldn't he get back there?" She has a great sense of fun.'

Despite her resilience, the trip was an exhausting one and Princess Anne undertook only one public engagement in the two weeks following her return. It was to the King's Troop Royal Horse Artillery barracks in St John's Wood. Visibility that morning was down to a few yards and fog drifting through the wrought iron gates swirled around the guard of honour in their musical comedy uniforms – all gold braid

on blue, busbies, tight trousers and gleaming swords. It was Princess Anne's first official visit to the King's Troop, established by George VI in 1947.

Major Malcolm Wallace, Commanding Officer, resplendent in frock coat, white gloves and dazzling boots and spurs, peered out into the fog. 'So many Rolls-Royces in St John's Wood. Gives you a heart attack.' He didn't seem too worried. He was, after all, expecting friends. Formalities would be observed today; it would be 'Your Royal Highness' and 'Ma'am' throughout, but as *chef d'équipe* of the British Three Day Eventing Team, he was more used to the camaraderie of 'Anne' and 'Mark'.

When her Rolls finally crept through the gates and the Bombardiers sprang to attention, Princess Anne emerged brisk and smiling. Unencumbered by an overcoat, despite the raw morning, she wore a sage green tweed suit, green silk shirt, matching turban and black accessories. Maureen Baker, ex-Susan Small, is one of her favourite designers and Princess Anne has said 'I'm rather conservative about clothes … a good suit goes on for ever, if it's made properly in the first place and has a sort of classic look about it.' Today's suit was well cut, accentuating her height and slimness as she turned away with Malcolm Wallace to inspect the officers' chargers, her tanned security man hovering ahead and Mark Phillips following a few paces behind, wearing a grey pin-striped suit and a slightly puzzled expression.

The chargers are the élite of the barracks, stabled in boxes rather than stalls and allowed to keep their manes unhogged and flowing. They seemed genuinely excited at the Royal approach, whinnying, pawing at their bedding with carefully oiled hooves and stretching out their well-groomed noses in hopes of a royal caress. Their minders stood rigidly to attention while the Princess asked them such typically practical questions as how long had they been with the Troop, or with their particular horse, and how much experience they had had with horses beforehand.

Although she looked pale, presumably still recovering from the African trip and the aftermath of a cold, she looked both interested and relaxed, as she tends to do in the company of horses and indeed of service people. About 30 of her 170 plus engagements in 1982 were connected with the services and a dozen each with Save the Children and her other favourite charity, Riding for the Disabled. The year also spanned four foreign trips (including a rather unhappy tour of Colorado and Texas where her public reaction to the birth of Prince William was undeniably terse) and saw an increasing involvement with London University where she succeeded the Queen Mother as Chancellor. When her parents were in Australia in October she carried out 15 public engagements in a week as well as other duties as Councillor of State which she has to take on when the Queen is out of the country. It is a schedule that would tax most politicians and businessmen but when she is interested she seems to thrive on the pressure. 'She's a workaholic', says Giles Witherington, Chairman of Save the Children. 'When I go to the Palace to brief her, she seems to know as much as I do.'

As the morning progressed at the Barracks, the sun broke through the fog, glinting on the gun carriages and the clipped coats of the horses in the manège. Whilst Princess Anne bent intently to examine the heavy harness with its welter of traces, her lady-in-waiting, Victoria Legge-Bourke, tall and blonde in emerald green suit and navy Sloane ranger velvet beret, talked to the Adjutant Captain Ian Vere Nicoll about the necessary temperament of a good line horse. Princess Anne has four ladies-in-waiting and two reserves, one of whom

is a close friend, Leonora Lichfield. They are all part-time, unpaid except for expenses, and count among her most valued companions. 'They must be good at chatting people up and be nice and bright and cheerful even when they don't feel like it,' she has said. 'You don't want someone looking ratty or glum.'

Within a few days, Victoria and the other ladies-in-waiting, together with Colonel Peter Gibbs, the Princess' Private Secretary, and her personal secretary Mrs David Hodgson, would attend a planning meeting at her apartments at the Palace to organize her engagements for six months ahead. All those present are either paid a salary or expenses from her annual £106,500 Civil List allowance, as are her

Husband and wife at the start of their day with the Beaufort (right). The Duke of Beaufort's Hounds, as the hunt is properly titled, are Mark's home pack. He has hunted with them since childhood.

Both Prince Charles's home, Highgrove, and the Michaels of Kent's, Nether Lypiatt, also lie in Beaufort country – leading the Queen to remark jokingly in conversation that Gloucestershire was becoming 'rather common'.

A poignant symbol of Princess Anne's affection for horses (below). Doublet was a favourite mount, a Christmas gift from the Queen in 1970, on which the Princess won the 1971 European Three Day Event title. Tragically the 11-year-old chestnut broke a leg on Smith's Lawn, Windsor, and had to be put down.

DOUBLET.
BORN · 9.5.63.
DIED · 13.5.74.
EUROPEAN
CHAMPION
1971

bodyguards and the basic staff necessary to run Gatcombe as her private home. She stresses that the Civil List money is expenses rather than pay and that 'I never have, and never will, spend a single penny of it on horses'.

Her passion for and rapport with horses is unquestionable. She won the 1971 European Horse Trials at Burleigh and represented Great Britain in 1973 at Kiev, in 1975 in Germany and in 1976 at the Montreal Olympics. She is a considerable athlete and she moves like one, walking and standing with assurance and precision.

She had undoubtedly enjoyed her morning with the King's Troop and was still animated and smiling as Malcolm Wallace escorted her and Mark Phillips in to the Officers' Mess for lunch.

'It will be traditional English grub,' one of the officers had told me, remembering, no doubt, that Princess Anne is known to dislike fancy food as much as she does smoking or the overimbibing of alcohol. According to her first cook at Gatcombe, 'They don't like rich food and eat merely plain things like roasts. Everything not eaten is used. Staff get leftovers and Anne and Mark are not above tucking into a cottage pie.' Anne herself explains that 'Economy is bred into me. I was brought up by my parents and nanny to believe things were not to be wasted.' Her cost-consciousness in furnishing Gatcombe frustrated David Hicks.

After lunch, it was back to Gatcombe

for a few more untypically quiet days. Gatcombe was bought by the Queen for a reputed £500,000 in 1976. It is a 35-roomed porticoed Cotswold stone house, set in parkland and 800 acres which Mark Phillips farms. It is a much valued retreat for the Princess who has said that the more you appear in public, the more you need 'an honest to goodness home life and proper privacy'. When she is at home, she says, she is just a farmer's wife, helping with the problems of the estate, driving into the local town in jeans and occasionally collecting her son Peter, aged five, from the

nearby school of Blueboys. Yet even at Gatcombe boxes arrive almost every day from the Palace with correspondence and queries on future engagements and these she attends to herself without the aid of a secretary.

On the Monday before her visit to the King's Troop she and Mark had spent a rare day out hunting with the Duke of Beaufort's hounds but the rest of the week was given over to entirely private activities, spending valuable time with Peter and Zara, now nearly two, hacking round the lanes on the two young horses she has on

Princess Anne inspects the Sword Guard as she pays her first official visit to the King's Troop Royal Horse Artillery, established by her grandfather King George VI in 1947. It was her one official event in an otherwise untypically quiet week, and her first public duty after an immensely successful but gruelling tour of Africa and the Middle East for the Save The Children Fund, of which she is President.

Escorted (left) by Captain Warwick Shaw of the King's Troop, Princess Anne begins her tour of the St John's Wood barracks. She is obviously at home in the company of military men and horses. In the Ceremonial Harness Room, she talks to Gunner Victor Hamilton (below) and seems generally interested and relaxed. More than twenty of the 170 engagements she undertook in 1982 involved the services. At St John's Wood, the men stood rigidly to attention while the Princess asked them straightforward questions such as had they had experience of horses before they joined the Troop? Mark Phillips, just visible in the background of the picture escorted by Staff Sergeant Tony Payne, followed a few paces behind looking slightly ill at ease.

trial to replace her previous eventer Stevie B, whose general 'peeriness', as she described it, led to a few mistakes at the water jumps and some of her more publicized falls, irritation at Press photographers and headlines in the populars like 'Anne – time for a swear box?' Most of the Phillips' friends who visit Gatcombe are from the farming or riding worlds. They stress the informality of the house, the preference for simple rather than grand entertaining, in what is very much a family home, complete with the clutter of small children and the three dogs – Laura, a lurcher, Random, a Gascony hound and Apollo, a cast-off corgi from the Palace.

The following week would be a more typical one, involving a visit to the North-East, an official lunch in London and a Save the Children reception at St James's Palace to thank a group of high-powered businessmen and industrialists for their financial help throughout the year. At the reception, the Princess looked rested by her spell in the country and recounted her African trip with enthusiasm. 'She sure knew about the Middle East' said James Dunlap, President of Texaco. 'Of course, she should have been an Ambassador,' said Mrs Neil Marten, wife of the Tory Minister and herself a member of the Save the Children Council. Victoria Legge-Bourke, who had been on part of the tour with the Princess, said that it had been such a success because Anne is 'always wholehearted in everything she does'.

Her bodyguard, Colin Tebbutt, rocking back on his heels sipping an orange juice, was as watchful as ever, even in the salons of St James's. 'She's a hundred per cent, this girl,' he said with pride. And as one regular Royal-watcher explained, 'A certain loyalty is expected from the entourage, but genuine respect tells you a lot more.'
Jane McKerron

Princess Anne shares a joke with Major Malcolm Wallace, Commanding Officer of the King's Troop, while behind them Mark Phillips talks to Captain Ian Vere Nicoll. As chef d'équipe of the British Three Day Eventing Team, Wallace not only knows the couple well (hence the invitation to visit the Troop in the first place) but in a different social context would call them 'Anne' and 'Mark'. On the day of the visit, however, formalities prevailed and it was 'Your Royal Highness' even in the Officers' Mess where the party retired later for a typically English lunch.

THE QUEEN MOTHER

At the Royal College of Obstetricians and Gynaecologists, the Queen Mother and the President, Mr Rustan Moolan Feroze, pass beneath a painting of the Queen officially opening the College in 1960. The Queen, the Queen Mother, and Princess Margaret are all Patrons of the College.

The Queen Mother has made it a policy throughout her public life never to admit to feeling cold, tired or ill, so it was no surprise to find her attending the inaugural meeting of the Court of Patrons of the Royal College of Obstetricians and Gynaecologists as planned, even though it was only eight days since the operation under general anaesthetic to remove a fishbone from her throat. It was only on the insistence of her doctors that she had agreed reluctantly to cancel her evening engagements for the week – the reception for the Diplomatic Corps at Buckingham Palace on Tuesday (she loves parties, and dancing Scottish country and ballroom) and the Royal Ballet's gala at Covent Garden on Thursday, one of her 'Hardy Annuals' – the engagements she likes to do every year if she can.

Late on Tuesday afternoon, the Queen Mother was driven to the Royal College in Regent's Park in her own Rolls-Royce (she also owns a Daimler) with her detective sitting beside the chauffeur, and her lady-in-waiting, Ruth, Lady Fermoy, and her private secretary, Sir Martin Gilliat, beside her in the back. (It's a bit of a squeeze, so on longer journeys Sir Martin travels in a separate car.)

It was her first public appearance since the operation, so the media were out in force – BBC, ITN, and a battery of photographers for whom, as usual, she stopped and posed, smiling to left, to centre and right. (She is far and away their favourite royal. 'She's always smiling,' said one old hand, 'and she knows exactly where to stop for us to get the best pictures.')

She looked rather pale and tired, not surprisingly, but though it was a cold night, she wore just a grey mink stole over a short, floaty turquoise and silver evening dress with matching, thick-heeled turquoise shoes – the sort of timeless, rather theatrical outfit (in fact she refers to her clothes as 'the props'), which has become her trademark. As always, she was wearing her three strings of pearls (she even wears them salmon fishing, along with a battered felt hat, waders and mac), and sapphire and diamond drop earrings. Her hair looked a little untidy, but it was probably so noticeable because she almost never appears in public without a hat, or a tiara.

It was a relatively short engagement – the presentation of a small bouquet, two brief stops to chat along the line of college staff in the hall, a dozen handshakes and lots of smiles around a horseshoe of gynaecological dignitaries, the opening session of the Court of Patrons behind closed doors, drinks with members and their wives (the Queen Mother likes gin and tonic with ice and lemon). She left after about an hour, stopping in the hall to chat briefly to a few of the staff, identifying all the flowers in her bouquet (she is a keen gardener), before driving back to Clarence House, probably for a quiet supper on a tray in front of the television.

If Wednesday was typical of other working days when the Queen Mother has no public engagements, she would have started work about ten, having read *The Times*, *Telegraph*, *Mail* and *Express*, and spent the morning writing personal letters, dealing with official correspondence and

The visit to the Royal College of Obstetricians (left) was the Queen Mother's first public engagement after she had an operation to remove a fishbone from her throat, so press photographers were out in force. They always speak of her admiringly and call her a 'real trouper'.

requests for visits. She is patron of some three hundred organizations and charities, colonel-in-chief of eight British regiments, commandant-in-chief of all three women's services and Warden of the Cinque Ports, so there is no shortage of invitations. She declines to nominate favourites, but anything to do with young people, or music, or medicine, is likely to get a sympathetic hearing. The Queen Mother sees every request that comes in, and with Sir Martin Gilliat, works out a programme for five or six months ahead. If she accepts an invitation some distance from London, her office will contact the county's Lord Lieutenant to see if there is something else she can open, unveil or visit while she is there.

She sometimes entertains family or friends for lunch, but if not, she will lunch with her Household—her lady-in-waiting (there are four, on a rota), her private secretary, her treasurer, her comptroller, her press secretary and possibly an equerry – all paid for, along with her domestic staff of about forty, from her Civil List allowance of £306,600.

If she doesn't see the Queen or Princess Margaret, she will speak to them on the phone. The operator on the Clarence House switchboard is said to put through calls to Buckingham Palace with 'Your Majesty? I have Her Majesty for you, Your Majesty'. She also walks her corgis, Blackie and Geordie every day, regardless of the weather.

In the afternoon, she may have a fitting

The Queen Mother meets Lord Matthews (left) and staff of Cunard on board the QE2 at Southampton. She unveiled a plaque in the Queen's Room commemorating the ship's part in the Falklands Campaign, and talked to men of the 5 Brigade who had served in the Falklands. The Queen Mother was on board the Royal Yacht *Britannia* in the Solent, when the QE2 returned from the South Atlantic and she arranged for *Britannia* to take part in the homecoming celebrations.

with her dressmaker or milliner – Evelyn Elliot, successor to Sir Norman at the House of Hartnell or Joy Quested-Nowell, from Rudolf in Mayfair, the firm which for years has made the off-the-face, flowered, feathered or veiled hats (some of the Queen Mother's favourites are now in their third or fourth incarnation) for which she is famous. She rarely ventures out to shop, apart from the occasional visit to Fortnum's just up the road, but sends her ladies-in-waiting, or has a selection of items sent round.

Tea is often a social occasion at Clarence House, with guests invited to a hearty Scottish spread between 5 and 6 pm. The Queen Mother also enjoys dinner parties, and has been known in recent years to persuade fellow guests (all of her own generation) at a private dinner party to roll back the carpet for an impromptu dance.

Thursday was a long day. The Queen Mother was driven to Buckingham Palace at 10.45 am, to board a red Wessex helicopter (her favourite form of transport, in spite of a forced landing in Windsor Great Park last summer) along with her usual retinue, plus an equerry, to fly to Southampton where she was to unveil a plaque on the *Queen Elizabeth II* to commemorate its part in the Falklands campaign.

She arrived just after half past eleven, smiling as always, dressed in a Gauloise blue dress and coat, with matching feathered, veiled hat. She began shaking hands at once – harbour officials, city officials,

The helicopter has been the Queen Mother's favourite form of transport ever since she made her first flight in 1955. She also enjoys ordinary flying and, in May 1952, took the controls of a Comet airliner on a proving flight across Europe. Afterwards she sent a telegram to No. 600 (City of London) Squadron Royal Auxiliary Air Force, of which she was honorary Air Commodore during the war, saying 'I am delighted to tell you that today I took over as first pilot of a Comet aircraft ... Thoughts turned to 600 squadron. What the passengers thought I really wouldn't like to say.'

Lord Matthews and staff from Cunard, the captain and some of the crew. At noon, she arrived in the Queen's Room to unveil the plaque, and proved that the Royal Handbag does have a function, by taking her speech out of it. She delivered it in a strong clear voice, pronouncing 'launched' in true naval fashion as 'lunched'.

Men from the 5th Parachute Brigade which had travelled to the Falklands aboard the QE2 were waiting to meet the Queen Mother, standing stiffly At Ease, hands behind their backs where their fingers were nervously trying to tie themselves in knots. Once she began talking to them, the knot-tying ceased and they soon began to chat and laugh. Noël Coward once said that the Queen Mother leaves behind her 'gibbering worshippers', and it's true. 'She's lovely!' 'Marvellous!' 'She really puts you at your ease', 'She's so *human*'.

Her handshake is very gentle, but not limp. She looks you straight in the eye and if the questions she asks are sometimes bland, she asks them with genuine interest. She listens to the reply, too, and often picks up on something that has been said rather than moving on to the next stock question. People who know her well say that she does have a genuine curiosity about people and things, and will always find something of interest in the most tedious occasion, or the most boring person. She also manages

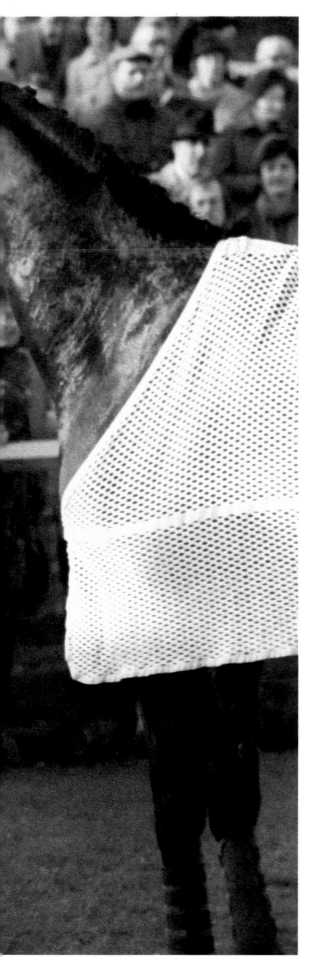

to imply that she's just like the rest of us – unlike other royals, she always talks about 'my daughter' or 'my grandson', not 'The Queen' or 'The Prince of Wales', and admits, as any mother would, that she finds it hurtful when her children are attacked by the Press. She sees the job she does as her duty – 'One does what one can for one's country' she has been heard to say, with total sincerity, but she never makes it seem like 'duty'. Instead, she manages to give the impression that there is nothing she would rather be doing.

Her stamina is legendary. From the time she stepped out of the helicopter until she sat down to lunch two hours later, she was on her feet, touring the ship, mingling with guests at a pre-lunch cocktail party, not simply waiting for people to be brought to her, but actively seeking them out.

She left twenty minutes late, and though there was a biting wind she wound down the window of the Rolls taking her from the ship to the helicopter, so that the small crowd waiting in the cold could see her smiling and waving. (She is said to have described her unique wave as like unscrewing the lid of a large jar of sweets!)

On Friday afternoon she paid a private visit, with Sir Martin Gilliat and a lady-in-waiting, to Sandown Park to watch her horse, Sun Rising, run in the 2 o'clock race, the Haig Whisky Novice Hurdles, and win £393 by finishing second. Steeplechasing is her great passion, and she has seven horses in training with Fulke Walwyn at Lambourn. If she is free during the week, and they are running at a course near London, she will go and watch. If not, she'll watch the race on television, or listen to 'the blower', the racing information service wired into betting shops, and into Clarence House, although she never bets.

From Sandown, she was driven to The Royal Lodge, Windsor, the favourite of her four homes (Clarence House, Birkhall, near Balmoral, and the Castle of May in Caithness, the only home she owns personally, are the other three) where she spends most weekends, often with Princess Margaret and a small group of friends, from Friday evening to Monday evening, engagements and fishbones permitting.

Gay Search

Racing at Sandown Park, where her horse, Sun Rising, came second in the Novice Hurdles. The Queen Mother's first venture in racehorse-owning was in 1949 when she and the Queen together bought the steeplechaser Monaveen. Since then her racing colours – pale blue shirt with buff stripes and pale blue sleeves and black cap with gold tassel – have been carried by many winning jockeys. But the greatest prize in steeplechasing – the Grand National – has always eluded her. In 1956 her horse Devon Loch, ridden by Dick Francis, was six lengths ahead with fifty yards to go when suddenly and inexplicably, he fell. The Queen Mother's response? A philosophical, 'That's racing.'

Royal Residences

Prince and Princess Michael of Kent joined 'royal Gloucestershire' in 1981 when they bought Nether Lypiatt Manor (below) near Stroud for £300,000. It has been called 'the most beautiful small house in Britain.'

Only 46 feet square, but four storeys tall, it stands on a hill and has twelve bedrooms, five bathrooms, and a heated swimming-pool. Another attraction for the Princess, a keen huntswoman, is that it lies in the heart of Beaufort country.

Gatcombe Park (below), in Gloucestershire, was bought by the Queen for Princess Anne and Captain Mark Phillips in 1976 for a reported £500,000. It is a two-storey Georgian house with a fine portico and conservatory, listed stables, and 730 acres.

Controversy rages about the high cost of policing Gatcombe – about £60,000 a year, of which half is paid by local ratepayers. The Gatcombe postman is quoted as saying: 'There are more police there than in the City of London. It's like Colditz.'

Barnwell Manor (below), in Northamptonshire, is the home of Princess Alice; her son, the Duke of Gloucester, farms its 2,500-acre estate. It is reckoned to be one of the most efficient agricultural units in the Midlands. The grey gabled stone house dates from Elizabethan times and has a ruined 13th-century castle nearby.

Highgrove (above) is the country home of the Prince and Princess of Wales, and was bought in 1980 for a reputed £800,000. It is a Georgian house with nine bedrooms, six bathrooms, heated swimming-pool, and 347-acre estate. The interior was designed by David Hicks. One of the disadvantages of Highgrove is that a public

footpath runs right through the grounds, and the house has been burgled three times in recent years. Security costs are therefore high – currently about £50,000 a year. The house contains a special steel-lined 'fortress' room, with reinforced walls, to which the Prince and Princess are supposed to retire in the event of a terrorist attack.

One of Prince Charles's possessions as Duke of Cornwall is 'Tamarisk' (right), a three-bedroomed bungalow on St Mary's in the Scilly Isles where ex-Prime Minister Sir Harold Wilson is a neighbour. The local people are famously discreet, so it is a popular royal hideaway.

Kensington Palace (below) is known by Prince Charles as 'the aunt heap' and indeed it does contain an extraordinarily large gathering of royal relatives – Princess Margaret, Princess Alice, the Gloucesters, the Michaels of Kent, and now the Prince and Princess of Wales at Nos 8–9. Despite perennial complaints of overcrowding and cramped quarters, there are considerable security advantages in having all the Royals corralled together in Kensington.

Birkhall (top right) is the Queen Mother's home at Balmoral, and noted for its fine salmon fishing. There is a story that Prince Charles once returned to Balmoral with a salmon he had caught at Birkhall. 'Did you have permission to fish there?' asked the Queen. 'Well, no,' said Charles. 'You do not live at Birkhall *yet*,' retorted the Queen, and made him take the fish back.

Clarence House (left) in St James's Palace, became the Queen Mother's London home on the death of her husband. It contains priceless china and paintings by Stubbs, Monet, Sickert and Augustus John. It also contains a 'Blower'—the bookmakers' information service. The system was installed in 1965 and a spokesman explained, 'The Queen Mother cannot always get to the races, and she does like to follow her horses' progress.'

Thatched House Lodge in Richmond Park (above) has been the home of Princess Alexandra and the Hon. Angus Ogilvy since their marriage in 1963, and both their children were born here. The house was built by Prime Minister Sir Robert Walpole in 1727, and its name is taken from the octagonal thatched gazebo (left) which stands in its three-acre grounds. It is surrounded by high fences to keep out the Park deer. Thatched House Lodge is now the only private house in Richmond Park. White Lodge nearby, which was the birthplace of the Duke of Windsor, is now the home of the Royal Ballet School.

PRINCESS MARGARET

Not everyone wears a mink to go to the supermarket but this was a special brand new Sainsbury's and a Very Special Shopper, who was clearly enjoying a somewhat unusual royal engagement.

There is a certain tinge of anxiety attached to a Princess Margaret occasion – what mood will she arrive in? She has occasionally been known to steam in with a barely concealed scowl and steam out again without speaking a syllable more than absolutely necessary. She has refused to meet a line-up of dignitaries because one of them incautiously referred to the Queen Mother as 'your mother'. It is not for nothing that she has the reputation of being the most difficult member of the Royal Family or that she recently scored even lower marks in the public popularity stakes than Princess Anne (the poll was a close thing).

But at present the stormy weather had receded from Kensington Palace. The Princess was clearly good-humoured all week. At fifty-two, she looks glamorous again in the way she used to do in the Fifties. Her shape is good, indeed provocative, her blue eyes flash back stunningly at the flashbulbs, her complexion is unflawed and her legs, when she shows them, are superb. A glance at foreign royalty shows that a highly ornamental princess is nothing to sneeze at.

There is no evidence for the suggestion that she is easing up on the job. She does an average of three days of public engagements a week. And being alone, she doesn't mind turning out at weekends. Her son David, Lord Linley, is cabinet-making in Surrey. Only her daughter, Lady Sarah Armstrong-Jones, who attends Camberwell School of Art, lives with her, at 1A Kensington Palace.

After thirty-five years the Princess doesn't draw large crowds in the streets but her presence guarantees a full house inside – and thereby the raising of large sums for the charities or pet projects she supports. People are eager to pay through the nose to be present at any do she attends. That is the reward for those who have worked hard or given generously. The magic wouldn't work if she were seen as the bored or ungracious Ugly Sister that she is sometimes held out to be.

Politicians at election time talk of their paw-shaking chores as 'pressing the flesh'. Princess Margaret dutifully presses it but she doesn't linger over it. If there's nothing to say after hello, she says nothing – and looks round for the next. As a result her visits usually finish on time, if not ahead of it. She doesn't shine at small-talk, like Prince Charles. She seldom talks to bystanders. If it's bitterly cold, she keeps moving. She was brought up in a time when royalty did not go overboard for public relations. It was sufficient for them simply to be seen.

Her week was a contrast between theatrical occasions, which she obviously enjoys, and a visit to a council estate in a tough area of Coventry, where her reception was rowdier but not, as some had feared, hostile. She appeared to enjoy that just as much – or was it the actress in her giving a performance?

You could not ask for a more royalist city than Bath, where she opened the magnificently restored Theatre Royal (built 1805). The carpenters, painters and vacuum cleaners were still at work almost up to the moment when her dark red Rolls-

The Princess unveils a plaque to celebrate the re-opening of the Theatre Royal, Bath. Painters, carpenters and cleaners had finished their work only minutes beforehand.

Royce (her own, she buys them) drew up to the portico lately vacated by a skip.

Awaiting her was her host for the night, her old friend Jeremy Fry, the chairman of the restoration appeal which is still trying to raise the last of the money. She spent an hour poking about from top to bottom, backstage and front, looking appreciatively up at the lights as she trod the new boards (the stage had holes in it when she last saw it). The horseshoe-shaped auditorium gleamed in white, gold and red thanks to another old acquaintance, Carl Toms, who also designed her drawing room car-. pet. 'We did it in red because you said so,' they told her.

She obviously loved the theatre – who wouldn't? – but there was a hint of mischief about her performance. 'And now I want you to meet someone else,' announced Mr Fry, shepherding her on to yet more handshakes. 'I wonder who that can be?' she asked with mock innocence. The posse of photographers were shooed back with a splintering of microphone booms against the low ceiling. '*Crunched* into a corner!' she said in her actressy voice, enjoying their predicament. At such moments it almost seems she might suddenly send the whole thing up and be chummy – but woe betide anyone who jumped to that conclusion. In public, the royal mystique must always be maintained.

It was only the beginning of a long night. Cohorts of worthies awaited her at the Assembly Rooms, then back to Mr Fry's house with just time to change for the performance – the National Theatre's visiting production of *A Midsummer Night's Dream* – into a turquoise and silver gown with a white mink jacket. After the show, another visit backstage to meet the stage staff ('Do you recycle all these leaves?') and then two after-theatre parties, greeting, greeting, greeting. At the last, at Mr Fry's house where she was staying the night, she met Paul Scofield and the cast. It went on long into the small hours and, being resident, she was there to the end. The Princess is an assiduous diary-writer, noting all she sees, but it is unlikely much got written that night.

Apparently unwearied, she was on duty the next morning visiting a new Sains-

Princess Margaret arriving at the Theatre Royal (below) for the gala opening night, and taking her seat (left) at the focus of the horseshoe-shaped theatre. A packed house at high prices helped raise some of the still-needed money for the Theatre appeal. The appeal was organized by the Princess's old friend, Jeremy Fry, who sits beside her, on her right.

bury's supermarket built behind a listed railway station, which Sainsbury's had restored to antique splendour as part of the development deal. Shops, however large, do not often figure in royal itineraries. By an interesting coincidence, Sainsbury's were the biggest contributor to the Theatre Royal's restoration fund.

You could hardly call her shopping call a get-together over the trolleys – that's not Princess Margaret's style. Anyway the backward-moving wall of photographers made such normality impossible, and there was Sir John Sainsbury diving into the deep freeze for meat for her inspection. Parsnips were admired and handled (they were very clean parsnips). Donning a crisp white coat, she observed the bakery and the jam-injecting process for the doughnuts.

The Princess walks through Bath's restored Victorian railway station with Sir John Sainsbury to visit his new supermarket. Her purchases in the shop – carried by a minion – were some butter, bacon and a hairbrush, and she stopped to admire the new weighing-machines at the checkout.

(Far right) Later the same day Princess Margaret travelled to Willenhall, Coventry, to celebrate the parish church's silver jubilee. She is greeted by a delighted vicar, the Rev. Stuart Hudson. 'Gives the place a bit of a lift in a difficult time,' he said afterwards.

Behind her walked an assistant carrying a wire basket for her purchases – a quantity of butter, streaky bacon and a small hair-curling brush.

Then it was a trek across foggy country to Warwickshire and another booted and spurred Lord Lieutenant, this one an Osbert Lancaster figure with a monocle. Lords Lieutenant are the essential oil in these visits – they forward the requests, vet the guest-list, arrange the ceremonial (such things as the Order of Cars bulk large). The Lord Lieutenant's wife may act as lady-in-waiting, holding the bouquet or the fur as required, as well as providing female company.

At Willenhall, Coventry, the church, a starkly modern barn designed by Sir Basil Spence, was celebrating its first twenty-five years. The vicar could hardly believe his luck when he got Princess Margaret for the service. He had, it is true, something special on his side. Willenhall was where the Princess used to visit a friend of her youth, the Rev. Simon Phipps, when he was an industrial chaplain and lived for years in one of the council flats. The Rev. – godfather to her son – is now the Right Rev. the Bishop of Lincoln and it was he who was preaching the sermon, a down-to-earth one on unemployment.

96

She fitted in a visit to the working men's social club, a cheery place where pints stood on any available surface. To the somewhat stunned pleasure of the members and onlookers, she wandered round the club lounge with a large whisky and her cigarette-holder, looking very much at home. She ended in the community centre where the Willenhall inhabitants (by no means all churchgoers) awaiting their buffet supper found themselves infiltrated by a royal and clerical invasion. 'Gives the place a bit of a lift in a difficult time,' said the vicar, after seeing her off towards her aircraft of the Queen's Flight. It was the end of a two-day stint that was exhausting by anyone's standards.

The next night was a charity gala given by the Royal Ballet, whose active President she has been since it received its charter in 1956. She arrived at the Royal Opera House in a dress of eau-de-nil satin, her hair freshly done at David and Josef. There was the line-up in the foyer, the entry to the royal box specially installed in the centre of the circle, the National Anthem, the applause from a standing house – then down to ballet with the opera glasses, a massive pair big enough for bird-watching.

Afterwards she went to the party in the Crush Bar. The sea of evening dress of the charity supporters, who had paid £50, £60 and £75 a seat (the charities were the Shaftesbury Homes and the Royal Ballet and Opera House Appeal) were varied by the jeans, open-necked shirts and scarves of the dancers. A last-minute notice on the company board had told them that Princess Margaret would like to see all of them there 'whatever you are wearing'.

It was Nureyev's evening – the première of his ballet, *The Tempest* – and he squired her into the party like a ballet partner. Still in costume and in his prop crown, he looked more imperial than the tiaraless Princess. The mask that often looks slightly

apprehensive behind the public smile had gone. She was among friends and bohemians. The difference was striking: she was the animated, talkative partygoer, enjoying stage talk and gossip, gesturing with her finger, whispering to Nureyev, joking with the corps and putting up her cheek for a kiss from the boys. 'We like her. She's a very nice woman,' said the dancers. Her programme scheduled her to be home at eleven. She didn't leave till almost midnight, having livened the party up considerably. A few days later, at the Friends of Covent Garden Christmas Party, held on the stage of Covent Garden,

At the Royal Opera House, Covent Garden, for a charity gala performance by the Royal Ballet, the Princess talks to disabled girls from The Shaftesbury Society, who presented her with a bouquet.

the Princess sat on some scenery clouds and was hoisted majestically up to the flies. Later, she came on stage in a carriage drawn by the boys of the Royal Ballet to lead the carol singing.

Had she not been born a princess, she might well have been an actress. She has been part of the royal show since 1947 – a long run. She injects vitality into any gathering, and gets what laughs there are to get, consonant with dignity. If her part is sometimes irksome – she might have done wonders with a bigger role – she is too professional to allow herself to show it.

Peter Lewis

For the party in the Crush Bar of the Opera House after the performance (insets below), the dancers were invited to 'come in whatever you are wearing', so jeans and sweaters mingled with evening dress. The Princess, watched by the Opera House's General Director, Sir John Tooley, makes a point to principal dancer Wayne Eagling; and listens to Rudolf Nureyev, still in his costume from *Raymonda*, one of the three ballets on the programme that evening.

THE DUKE OF KENT

**In his robes as Chancellor
of the University of Surrey,
the Duke presides over a
degree-giving ceremony at
Guildford Cathedral.**

The week started well for HRH The Duke of Kent. No member of the Royal Family is as passionately fond of music as he (not excluding Prince Charles and his youthful cello), and certainly none is as genuinely well informed. The Duke is especially devoted to opera, reputedly knowing as much about Wagner as does Bernard Levin (though he talks about it less), and visiting the Bayreuth Festival regularly. So it was by no means an ordeal for him to attend a rare performance of Mahler's Eighth Symphony at the Royal Albert Hall on Sunday evening, arranged by Book Club Associates. Even had he not been in the Royal Box, the Duke would have sat in the audience anyway, and not only because his wife was one of seven hundred singers in the choirs. This was probably why it was easy to engage his formal participation at the last minute, only four weeks before the event. The calendar is normally full far in advance of this.

At the reception afterwards (which the photographer and I were told we could attend as long as we did not eat anything) we noticed how astonishingly relaxed the Duke was, whether talking to people at his table, or being presented, hands thrust in jacket pockets, to soloists.

His endearing affability is a lesson to the arrogant or the less experienced. Many of those who curtsey before him he greets by their first names. He is the most unpompous of royals, tolerant of those who may say or do the wrong thing in a moment of fear, and angry only with those who ought to know better; he knows the difference between rudeness and *naiveté*. One businessman, charmed into thinking this was almost as easy as having a pint at the pub, virtually slapped the Duke on his back. There was no icy stare, no sudden retreat into ceremony. Even with close friends and intimates, the Duke positively discourages malicious gossip and therefore never hears unkind remarks about people. It is a useful inhibition, commanding a respect which does not have to be manufactured.

The Duke of Kent's air of calm hides a man who is essentially shy and has had to learn to place people at their ease when he himself was anxious. He was deeply miserable at school and afflicted by severe sinus trouble. His guardian, King George VI, was not always as sympathetic as he might have been, and young 'Prince Eddy' often suffered from loneliness. On the other hand, Lord Mountbatten was a profound influence and kindly counsellor. Strength and confidence came to him at Sandhurst, a period of his life which changed him fundamentally.

On Monday morning, the Duke presided as Grand Master of the United Grand Lodge of England at the installation of his brother, Prince Michael of Kent, as a Provincial Grand Master. Oddly enough, this was one of the few occasions when the brothers met. It comes as a surprise to discover how little members of the Royal Family see of one another. They appear to operate in separate compartments, rushing from one appointment to the other and hardly ever crossing paths. There are strangers who have been invited to Buckingham Palace, Clarence House or St James's more often than members of the family.

The Duke of Kent has a session with his Private Secretary three times a year, at which all invitations are considered and the programme for the next four months is planned. The Duke not surprisingly prefers to attend those functions which suit his talents best: musical, military, and export.

The Freemason event was smothered in masonic secrecy, and the Duke went in by a back entrance. But our photographer, Jennifer Beeston, managed to catch him afterwards at the celebratory lunch in the Connaught Rooms. By this time he was used to seeing her pop up in front of him like a catapult. 'You must have run like a hare,' he said. She was unable to cover the next engagement, when the Duke attended a lecture at the Institution of Mechanical Engineers, which gave rise the next day to a cheerful salute: 'We missed you last night!' It was the first time any of his entourage can recall the Duke of Kent giving acknowledgement to a photographer. He even opened the door to call her.

The 'we' he used was not royal pretension. The Duke is always accompanied by his equerry, Captain Stewart, or his Private Secretary, Sir Richard Buckley, plus a personal security officer provided by Scotland Yard. There is sometimes a chauffeur, in any one of three cars, and sometimes the Duke drives himself; he is very attached to engines.

On Tuesday there was a long journey into the far reaches of North London to open the new test centre of MK Electric. As President of the British Computer Society, the Duke is fascinated by modern technology. Every minute was carefully timed (the tour was rehearsed by stand-ins), and the unveiling of the plaque was preceded by a nervous address by the managing director (who nearly called him 'Your Riyal Hoyness') and a brief, unhesitant and impressive reply by the Duke.

The organizers had allowed two minutes' conversation for each of the six people being presented. The PR man hovered in the background trying to signal one particular bore to shut up, but the Duke chatted on amiably, always showing interest, never showing tiredness. ('The Royal Family is *never* tired,' said Queen Mary.)

Far left: The Duke and his brother, Prince Michael, emerge from a masonic ceremony at Freemasons' Hall. The Duke of Kent has been Grand Master (ie head) of the Masons since 1967. Other royal masons have included King Edward VII, the Duke of Windsor, King George VI and Prince Philip, but so far Prince Charles remains a notable exception.

Left: The Duke with Sir George Edwards on his right and Lord Caldecote on his left at the Institution of Mechanical Engineers. (The model is of Jodrell Bank radiotelescope.) The Duke had invited himself along to hear his friend Sir George, former Chairman of the British Aircraft Corporation, give a lecture on British Aerospace.

After hearing his wife sing with the Bach Choir, the Duke went on to a reception afterwards at the Royal College of Music. The most musical of all the Royals, he is a keen opera buff and his car radio is permanently tuned to Radio 3.

Above: **The Duke is Chairman of the European Music Year Committee at the Arts Council and here confers with Secretary Ian Keith (left) and Chairman of the Music Panel John Manduell (right).**
Top: **Unveiling a plaque to commemorate the opening of MK Electric's new test centre in north London. As President of the British Computer Society, the Duke was delighted to be shown all the latest microcomputers and said afterwards, 'It's good to see a firm with confidence.'**

The only slight hint of possible impatience is his habit of playing with a large gold ring on his little finger, but he is never overtly bored.

By design, there is not much to eat. If all the chefs who want to produce their masterpiece for a royal guest were allowed to do so, we should have a very fat Royal Family. Things to nibble are the order of the day. Besides which, it is easier to talk, and talking is very much a part of the royal job. Faced with a man who is tongue-tied, the Duke often opens a conversation with 'I gather that . . .', using information which has been 'gathered' by Sir Richard Buckley and mugged up by the Duke in the car.

There are no embarrassing pauses.

From North London straight to Buckingham Palace for the awarding of South Atlantic medals, in company with the Prince of Wales and Prince Philip. The Duke is at home on a military occasion, and was very unhappy when he had to leave the army because the Government would no longer allow the ordinary tours of duty in Northern Ireland. He still relishes any military engagement.

The Duke's taste in suits echoes a habit of military precision – very neat, even natty, and perfectly tailored – while his Jermyn Street striped shirts seem to have rather more stripes, in slightly brighter

One of the graduates at the University of Surrey degree-giving ceremony was an Arab princess, and the head of her family, His Highness Sheikh Abdullah Al-Mubarak Al-Sabah, paid to have the whole event videorecorded. Afterwards he chatted to the Duke over a cup of tea.

to be with his family. When he accepted the position of Chancellor of the University of Surrey, he discovered that the degree ceremony usually took place on a Saturday. Tactfully he saw to it that the occasion was moved to a Friday, as he cherishes the weekends at home with his children (in Norfolk) and avoids public engagements which threaten to interrupt the weekend. If he does take a duty which comes during the holiday, he will travel by the fastest possible route, even if it means a helicopter, and has been angered by tittle-tattle which chastised him for wasting money.

The last two appointments of the week were a committee meeting at the Arts Council (the Duke is Chairman of the UK Committee for European Music Year) and a colourful ceremony at Guildford Cathedral when, as Chancellor of the University of Surrey, the Duke conferred degrees upon graduate students and four honorary recipients for two and a half hours, ending with a speech, written by himself, which was delivered with finer breath control and more articulacy than many of the assembled dons could muster. He contrived to mention the hardship suffered as a result of cuts in university funding, which left little doubt where his sympathies lay.

Quite apart from his royal duties, the Duke of Kent also has a job, as Vice-Chairman of the British Overseas Trade Board, and his commitments there occupy the largest single chunk of his working life. He is responsible for liaison with Area Advisory Boards and travels up and down the country several times a month, and abroad more than once a year. He is the only member of the Royal Family to have visited Communist China, and has also travelled extensively in West Africa. One gets the impression that the Duke will go anywhere if it is likely to improve the prospects for British exports, and he is constantly spilling out ideas for the export drive. An export salesman, he says, must have the feet of a policeman, the stamina of a horse, the endurance of a camel. He must also be an accomplished linguist, as the Duke himself is. There are many people in the BOTB who insist that the Duke of Kent is one of the unsung heroes of the Royal Family.
Brian Masters

colours, than those worn by other men. A dandy locked inside a conservative.

About three evenings a week are free of official appointments to spend quietly at home in York House with the Duchess. Staff there consists of a housekeeper, a maid and a valet. There are no more kitchen staff, and only three dailies who come in to do the dusting. It is much more modest than one would expect. The office employs, apart from Sir Richard Buckley, two secretaries and a part-time accountant (plus three ladies-in-waiting for the Duchess) who are paid from the Civil List allowance of £113,000 a year.

The Duke of Kent's greatest happiness is

THE DUCHESS OF KENT

The Duchess of Kent is a
fine second soprano and
joined the Bach Choir,
after an audition five years
ago. Tonight Mahler's
'symphony of a thousand'
is being performed at the
Royal Albert Hall. She is
passionate about music
and is often seen at
concerts.

HRH the Duchess of Kent comes from a Yorkshire family with a fine tradition of fête-opening and fund-raising. Like the Queen Mother, she now seems almost more whole-heartedly royal than those born to the job. As well as working for seemingly every charity to do with the sick, the dying, the crippled, the insane, the elderly and the helpless, the Duchess is Controller Commandant of the WRAC, Honorary Colonel of several regiments and Chancellor of Leeds University. She is a qualified Samaritan, having insisted on doing the training when she became patron, and while she is not allowed to go on duty, she has been known to pop into a branch and announce: 'Hello, I'm Katherine 1500' – her Samaritan number.

With two homes to run (a working apartment in York House, St James's, and a Georgian house, Anmer Hall, in ten acres of Norfolk countryside) and three children (the twenty-year-old Earl of St Andrews is at Cambridge, Lady Helen Windsor is at a London crammer, and Lord Nicholas Windsor is still at day school), the Duchess does not have much time to relax.

She rarely reads a book right through, doesn't watch much television, and isn't particularly sporting or athletic. She enjoys concerts and small dinner parties – where her guests are as likely to come from the arts as Debrett – and she is an accomplished pianist and organist. She has a fine soprano voice – a fact which can be verified on public platforms when the Duchess is the only one not merely mouthing the national anthem – and her greatest joy and hobby is singing with the Bach Choir.

So her week began happily, on Sunday, when she joined the Bach Choir for a performance of Mahler's Eighth, his 'symphony of a thousand' at the Royal Albert Hall. There were some 700 singers and 300 musicians on stage, and the Duchess appeared as a chic black speck among the second sopranos, her long blonde hair tied back in a pony tail. During the interval, her detective, who had been hanging about in the aisle, handed her a Harrods plastic bag. She disappeared into a corner of the corridor with two friends, sat down and unpacked a Thermos of coffee and three cups.

There was a reception after the performance at which her husband, the Duke, was guest of honour, but the Duchess did not go. She was hoarse after all her singing and wanted to be well rested for her engagement next day at Leeds University.

Her task at Leeds was to confer an honorary degree of Doctor of Law upon Herr Willy Brandt, the German ex-Chancellor. Willy Brandt gave a lecture about the survival of the human race. The Duchess made a neat speech in reply which she read from typed cards. Later she tugged at the robes of the President of the Union, Mary Cassidy, and said 'Hello, how are *you*? What did you think of my speech? Will the students approve of it?' Mary said later that even the most radical students approve of their Chancellor: 'She bothers to come to our lectures and societies and finds out what we think.'

Next day the Duchess was due to open Helen House, a hospice for dying children, in Oxford. 'I've been to so many hospices,' she confides, 'but this is the first children's

one and it is *so* important. I don't really know how it will affect me.' The Duchess had a nervous breakdown five years ago, after a miscarriage at the age of forty-four, and it is an understatement when she says, 'I'm not very robust.'

Within seconds of walking into Helen House, the Duchess was down on the floor chatting to three-year-old Catherine Worswick who presented the bouquet. 'Would you like a flower? Which one would you like? Ooooh you've chosen the biggest. Are you going to wear it or put it in a vase?' 'In a vase,' said the child, who had been speechless with nerves all morning.

The Duchess visited ten-year-old Re-becca, who has a progressive degeneration of the brain. 'Becky was so poorly when the Duchess came into the room,' her mother said afterwards. 'She said "Can you look at me, Rebecca?" and I turned her little face towards the Duchess. She said, "What a pretty dress – did Mummy make it?" and then she gave Rebecca a flower and said: "Perhaps Mummy will put it in water." I didn't really want to come today, but I thought it would be nice for Becky to meet the Duchess. Well . . . she didn't know she was meeting her, of course, but it was nice for her anyway.'

The Duchess lingered longer than she should in each of the children's rooms.

'This is not something that can be slotted into a schedule,' she explained. Her lady-in-waiting darted through to brief the policeman with the walkie-talkie that they were running late – 'It's going to be one of our *shorter* lunches today.' They cut the rest period to ten minutes but were still 45 minutes late for the nurses' prizegiving in the nearby Nuffield Orthopaedic Centre.

The welcoming committee, hustling the Duchess through to the hall, suddenly stopped in their tracks when they found she was no longer with them. She had recognized a porter holding open a door – 'How very nice to see you again, Mr Walker,' she said, 'and thank you for being

'By virtue of the authority vested in me . . .' The Duchess, as Chancellor of Leeds University, confers an Honorary Degree on Herr Willy Brandt (right), before posing for an official photograph (above). Afterwards, there is an informal supper and the Duchess leaves late. 'She is always behind schedule,' say patient police, 'She insists on talking to everyone.' The Duchess visits the University regularly, sits in on lectures, attends major Council and Senate Meetings: 'She is no mere figurehead,' says Vice Chancellor William Walsh.

so patient and waiting for me.'

On Wednesday and Thursday there were no official engagements – time to deal with correspondence, write speeches, have a briefing on future engagements, meet up with the directors and chairmen of her charities. The Duchess has decided to stop going to hospices for six months or so: 'If you do too many, you can't give enough to them.' She has a small staff – a personal secretary, three part-time ladies-in-waiting, and shares the services of the Duke's private secretary, Sir Richard Buckley.

If they are both home at lunch-time, the Duke and Duchess usually share an omelette or scrambled eggs, then she may go shopping, get her hair done, catch up with

did no such thing – she was out of her car and into the crowd in minutes, with the police in hot pursuit.

She toured the new burns unit, talking to people who had been so badly burned that their faces were scarcely human, then, later, she stood in a room full of geriatric patients who had been wheeled in to see her. Her smile was overwhelming, enveloping every person there: '*Thank* you for coming to see me,' she said. 'It has been such a treat for me to meet you all'.

The Duchess was, of course, late for lunch at the Basildon Development Corporation and as elusive as ever during a tour of the Marconi Avionics factory. As the managing director snapped at his staff,

friends. David, of David and Josef, a modest salon behind Berkeley Square, shampoos her hair twice a week and combs it out in between. When the Duchess (or Princess Margaret, who favours Josef) comes into the salon she sits in a certain chair and a junior pulls a string to form an instant screen of discreet venetian blinds.

At 8 am on Friday, David went to York House to fix the Duchess's hair under a tiny hat, for her visit to St Andrew's Hospital, Essex. The visit was over-policed, over-organized: 'The Duchess will alight here ... she will shake hands with the Lord Lieutenant there ...' Of course the Duchess

telling them to keep quiet, get the Press out of the way, open the doors, the Duchess had disappeared onto the shop floor: 'Oh, she's not meant to go *there*,' wailed a distraught official, 'we haven't cleaned those floors.'

On Friday evening the Duke and Duchess took off for a peaceful weekend in the country. On Sunday afternoon Princess Margaret's lady-in-waiting rang to say the Princess had 'flu. Could the Duchess possibly take over for her that evening and attend a gala performance at the Theatre Royal, Norwich? Of course.
Shirley Lowe

'Which flower would you like?' The Duchess of Kent helps three-year-old Catherine Worswick to relax at the opening of Helen House near Oxford, the world's first hospice for children (above left). 'I didn't know how it would affect me,' she said. Equally harrowing was a visit to a new regional burns unit at St Andrew's Hospital, Billericay (above right). 'The Duchess is wonderful with the old, the sick and children,' says an aide. 'She prefers meeting people to looking at machines.'

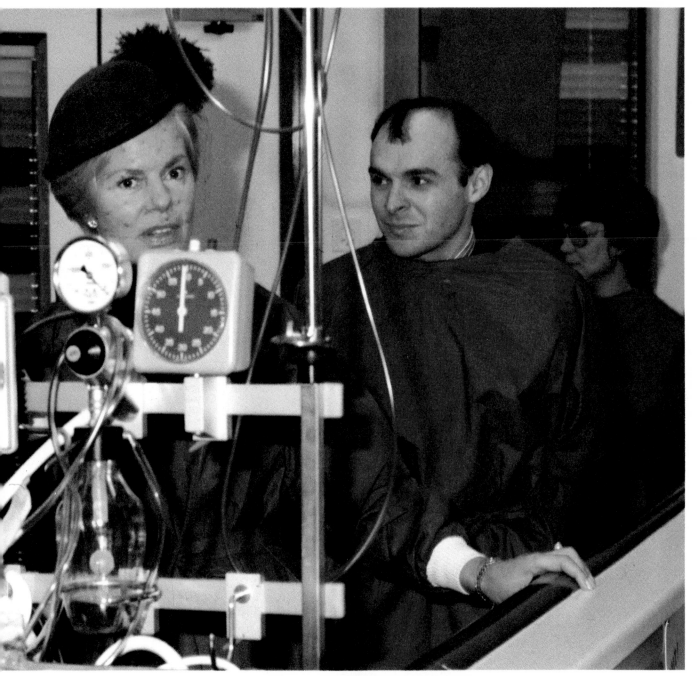

'Please forgive me for being so late, but I was somewhere you couldn't fit into a schedule.' The Duchess arrives at the Nuffield Orthopaedic Centre (left) after over-running the time set aside for the children's hospice. As Patron, she was presenting prizes at the annual prize-giving ceremony. She had a different question for each nurse and said: 'I hope you'll learn as much about men as about nursing,' to the nurse who had chosen *Manwatching* as her prize book.

PRINCESS ALICE AND THE DUKE AND DUCHESS OF GLOUCESTER

Princess Alice is grown
rather than born Royal.
Daughter of the 7th Duke
of Buccleuch, she was
educated at a top girls'
school, 'finished' in Paris,
and made her début at
Court.

The Duke and Duchess of Gloucester, and the Dowager Duchess
Princess Alice, divide their lives
amicably between two homes. Princess
Alice presides over Barnwell Manor, the
2,500-acre Northamptonshire estate which
her late husband, Prince Henry, bought in
the 1930s, while her son and daughter-in-
law make their home at Kensington Palace.
But, in practice, the young Gloucesters stay
with Princess Alice at Barnwell most weekends, and Princess Alice stays with them at
Kensington Palace whenever she has engagements in London during the week.

Princess Alice is the widow of a royal
prince, daughter-in-law to George V,
sister-in-law to George VI, and aunt to our
reigning Queen. As such, she receives a
£42,000 pa Civil List pension. Her son, the
Duke, receives a Civil List allowance of
£83,900 to pay for the expenses of the Kensington Palace staff. The staff consists of a
full-time equerry, Sir Simon Bland, with
two secretaries, an assistant, six ladies-in-
waiting who work on a rota, a cook, butler,
footman and nanny. The shortfall between
the allowance and the Kensington Palace
running costs is made up from the income
of the Barnwell estate.

At Barnwell, Princess Alice is very much
the lady of the manor. She attends the parish church every Sunday, joins in village
fêtes and jumble sales and, on this particular
Tuesday, accompanied the village school
to its annual Christingle service. Then she
came down to London to take up her
official life. At eighty-one, she might be
expected to ease up on her official engagements, but she nevertheless carried out

forty-six such duties last year, and remains
loyal to the seventy-four organizations of
which she is President or Patron.

Thus, on Wednesday evening, she attended a reception at the Tower of London
given by the Royal Green Jackets Ladies'
Guild, a charitable organization of past
and present officers' wives. Before the
party, she had her hair done, then, wearing
a chiffon and velvet black cocktail dress,
she was driven with her lady-in-waiting,
Miss Jane Egerton-Warburton, to the
Tower. Characteristically, she sat upright
in the car, her back not touching the seat.
Princess Alice, thanks perhaps to those de-
portment lessons years ago at St James
School, West Malvern, when she was Lady
Alice Montagu Douglas Scott, has an
upright carriage in all circumstances – the
perfect posture proof against time itself.

The next day, Thursday, she visited the
Park Lane Fair, an enormous mêlée of
stalls, in aid of the Forces Help Society and
Lord Roberts' Workshops. In a ballroom
crowded with hundreds of shoppers,
Princess Alice was a tiny figure, wearing a
beige coat, maroon dress with diamond
brooch at the throat, small maroon hat and
matching shoes. Unlike the Queen Mother,
Princess Alice favours subdued colours and
tailored elegance, which she finds at
Franka, a couture dressmaker in Dover
Street.

Behind the Princess came a retinue of
worthies including the charity appeals or-
ganizer, Mrs Anne Finlay, in charge of a
wicker basket borrowed from the Lord
Roberts Workshop stall. (On Friday, Princess Alice popped into the Lord Roberts

Scarlet uniforms and royalty have a natural affinity. When Sergeant J. McClellan and two other Chelsea Pensioners presented a bouquet at the Park Lane Fair, Princess Alice lingered a little longer and more warmly than elsewhere. As Colonel-in-Chief to three British Regiments and Deputy-Colonel-in-Chief of one more, she gives half a dozen audiences every year to senior officers. By courtesy consulted about senior appointments, she is closely in touch. At Christmas there is a card for each officers' mess and – arguably more important – a card for each sergeants' mess.

Workshop to return the basket herself.) Into it went the Princess's purchases – two jars of honey, a teddy bear, a nailbrush, a wind-up butterfly and a 'wonder growing' frog. Royalty does not carry money, so each purchase was carefully noted down for the bill to be sent to Kensington Palace later. The frog and teddy may well have been destined for the occupants of the Prince William cot at the Royal Free Hospital and the Princess Alice bed in a Solihull children's home. Princess Alice sends Christmas presents to each annually, having checked beforehand the name, age and sex of the child.

In an hour of tireless handshaking, Princess Alice smiled and talked to at least 120 helpers, including one pleased middle-aged lady who blurted out, 'I'm not a helper, just a person, but my name is Alice too.' The Princess showed the valuable royal skill of remembering faces – she recognized one of the stallholders, a Mrs Robin Allen, whom she had not seen since she was a child.

Other Royals crack jokes. Princess Alice does not try to. She shows tiny nervous mannerisms – shifting from one foot to another, clasping her hands – which disappear as her smile breaks through. The questions are the safe royal ones, but she listens intently to the answers.

Princess Alice is a conscientious, but singularly unobtrusive, member of the Royal Family. Her work is appreciated by the many organizations with which she is connected, but the public at large know little about her. The same might be said of her son Richard, the Duke of Gloucester, and his Danish-born wife, Birgitte. Either of them can walk down the street without being recognized and their public image is negligible. Yet, between them, they are patron or president of seventy-odd organizations, and they normally carry out four or five official engagements a week – they would carry out more, but they lack the staff to do the backup paperwork.

Richard of Gloucester is the first white-collar worker in the Royal Family. He is a qualified architect who, if his brother William had not died in an air crash in 1972, would have remained an upper middle class professional. He went to

Magdalen College, Cambridge, where he was known as Proggie to his friends (PROG = Prince Richard of Gloucester), then with two fellow-architects, Bernard Hunt and John Thompson, he set up Hunt Thompson Associates in Camden, north London. He bought a house overlooking the canal, cycled to work, and put Richard Gloucester on his business card. He dealt mainly with conversions for local authorities and housing associations. In July 1972 he married Birgitte van Deurs, a Danish secretary whom he had met on his second day at Cambridge. 'The Prince and the Commoner', said the headlines.

Six weeks later, Richard's elder brother William died and in 1974 on the death of his father, Richard became Duke of Gloucester. In 1978 he gave up his architectural partnership to become a full-time Royal and farmer. But he has sometimes chafed at the fact that, as a Royal, he is expected to be decorative rather than functional. 'Royalty must be professional ignoramuses,' he complained in 1979. 'It's a shame.'

At thirty-seven, the Duke has the obligatory Royal haircut, wears horn-rimmed spectacles, and a shy smile. He looks like a self-effacing, slightly troubled, City stockbroker. The Duchess, thirty-six, still looks as she did when she married – a candidate for the title of most popular girl in the school. She tries to work two weeks on and one week off, the off week being devoted to their three children – Alexander, Earl of Ulster, who is eight, Lady Davina Windsor, five, and three-year-old Lady Rose. The Gloucesters employ a full-time nanny but, if they are not working, they ferry the children to teaparties and dance and music classes themselves. The children are not corralled in the nursery but allowed to roam free. 'Sometimes,' says Sir Simon Bland, the Gloucesters' equerry, 'one feels as if one is working in a creche.' He says it amiably, with a touch of pride. In most royal households, members of staff have to make an appointment to see their employer, but Sir Simon and the senior lady-in-waiting, Louise Wigley, 'just pop upstairs and butt in. The Gloucesters are very tolerant. They never seem to mind very much.'

Upright in her official car (right), the Princess drives to the Tower of London for a reception given by the Royal Green Jackets Ladies' Guild. Below: Among the upmarket jumble of the Park Lane Fair. Princess Alice is escorted by its Chairman, Lady Norton and, on the right, Mrs Martin Pulling, in charge of the 'Once worn' boutique.

Every day a separate programme is issued for each of the Gloucesters and the children 'so that everyone knows where everyone is'. The Duke's working week began on Monday with a committee meeting for the Prince Albert Exhibition which he was helping to organize. The Duke is far from being merely a token Royal in this exercise: 'He always does his homework thoroughly,' reports Hermione Hobhouse, the exhibition's researcher. On Tuesday, he went by motorbike to another committee meeting – this one at the Design Centre to adjudicate product design.

On Thursday, he attended the inaugural meeting of the German Historical Institute at its new home in Bloomsbury Square. The Institute is funded by Volkswagen, and Volkswagen executives, as well as German diplomats, academics and politicians, were out in force. Presumably the Duke of Gloucester was selected as the appropriate Royal for this occasion because, as an architect and keen conservationist, he could be expected to appreciate the careful renovation of the house, once the home of the 18th-century architect John Nash.

The meeting began with informal chit-chat in the library. Chit-chat is not the Duke of Gloucester's forte: he prefers serious discussion. When one of the guests commented that the Institute was looking forward to joining the Bloomsbury community, the Duke told him rather pedantically, 'Well of course the myth is that Bloomsbury ever *was* a community. It wasn't.' The guest looked duly nonplussed.

Then Duke and guests sat down to listen to the speeches – seven speeches and one lecture, lasting altogether for 90 minutes. It was only in the 66th minute of this regal SAS course that the Duke began to show slight strain. He leant forward to contemplate his shoes intently and from then on looked up every ten minutes or so like a bewildered mole who had taken the wrong tunnel and was surprised by what he saw.

The Duke's own speech – which he wrote himself, as he always does – was the best. It was short, funny and confident. It contained one compliment, one plug for the Prince Albert Exhibition, and one mild joke – 'I come from a family who for two centuries regarded Germany as a suitable

The Duke of Gloucester meets German diplomats and academics (above), and gives a speech (right) at the inaugural meeting of the German Historical Institute, in Bloomsbury Square. As an architect and keen conservationist, the Duke was properly appreciative of the careful restoration of the house, which once belonged to architect John Nash.

source of breeding stock.' After the speeches, the Duke inspected all four floors of the Institute, staying 20 minutes longer than scheduled, then rushed home for a television programme on Nepal, one of his favourite countries. As always, he changed from his on-duty uniform of pin-striped suit, into his off-duty uniform of cords and sweater.

On Friday, the Duke received two members of the Bulldog Manpower Services – a prisoners' rehabilitation scheme – and then took his wife and mother, Princess Alice, to watch the school play of his son Alexander. Then the family all decamped for the weekend to Barnwell, where the Duke spent Saturday shooting, while Princess Alice resumed her quiet manorial round.

Off duty, the Gloucesters live the life of any well-to-do aristocratic family. Princess Alice is the country lady of the manor, presiding over fêtes and flower shows; the Gloucesters are young Knightsbridge, with a wide circle of friends from Cambridge, the world of architecture and design. The Duke dislikes the taste of alcohol so the Duchess does all the wine-buying and has become an amateur vintner. They eat simply, watch light comedy and environmental programmes on television. The Duke takes design, farming and architectural magazines – other magazines only come his way when they are provided on the Queen's Flight. His free time is devoted to model-making (planes, trains and ships) and photography – he has done the photography for three books and also acted as official photographer when Lady Rose was born. He has a large appetite for military history (though never himself a soldier) and has read every book on the Falklands War so far published.

The Duchess enjoys ballet, skiing and tennis. She has her hair done at Riché in Hay Hill and her clothes made at Franka in Dover Street (as does her mother-in-law). She buys two new outfits in summer and two in winter plus an evening gown (starting price for made-to-measure, £700). She is Patron, President or Commandant of over thirty organizations. 'When you're with her,' says Jessica Howey, fund-raiser for the Notting Hill Housing Trust, of which the Duchess is patron, 'you have no feeling of distance. She finds something different to say to everyone and I die a thousand deaths because people get so familiar.' One reason why people get so familiar is that they often do not recognize her – at a musical lecture on Bach a woman came up to her and chatted for five minutes without realizing her identity. 'What she loves,' says one who knows the Duchess well, 'is to gracefully climb over the fence which separates Us and Them. A British person who married into Royalty probably would have tried to widen the gap.'

The Duke is similarly unpretentious and hard-working. He is head of forty-seven organizations some of which – like the presidency of the National Association of Boys' Clubs – he inherited from his father, others of which reflect his own interests. 'He doesn't wait to be approached,' says David Simpson, Director of the anti-smoking campaign, ASH, of which the Duke is patron, 'he contacts us. If I give him speech notes, he always adds to them.' When the Duke went on a trade mission to China in 1980, he got his secretary to send ASH some Chinese stamps marking the World Health Organization's Anti-Smoking day. 'It's that kind of detail which makes you feel he sees us as something more than just a cause.' On their first meeting, David Simpson gave the Duke a T-shirt emblazoned, 'Kiss a non-smoker. Taste the difference.' 'That,' said the Duke, at a time when Prince Charles was still single, 'I should give to my cousin.' And he did.

The Duke and Duchess are aware that they are regarded as the Duke and Duchess of Invisibility. That bothers them less than whether they have done a good job. 'How did it go?' they usually ask after an engagement. If an award for 'Young Royals of the Year' existed, it is said that the Queen would have given it to the Gloucesters. She recognizes them as workers. In a time when Royalty is under more and more pressure to appear relevant to 'real' life, the Gloucesters have achieved it better than most. 'In the Royal industrial plant,' says a close observer, 'you could say the Gloucesters are middle management executives on the way up.'

Celia Haddon and **Yvonne Roberts**

PRINCESS ALEXANDRA

Princess Alexandra chats
with town and gown
(northern division) at the
Sugar House, Lancaster.
Her present poise is a far
cry from the almost
crippling shyness of her
youth. As a schoolgirl she
sobbed with
embarrassment when she
realized that a film of the
Queen's wedding was to
be shown in the main hall.
She didn't want her friends
to see her as a bridesmaid.
The headmistress allowed
her to absent herself from
the screening.

Princess Alexandra could be described as one of the world's very few professional cousins. Being a cousin of the Queen is her full-time job, the overriding factor in her life which dictates how she dresses (with quiet glamour), how she talks (with disarming blandness) and with whom she can be friends (only the discreet need apply). Her days are planned for her three months ahead. Every visit, every opening ceremony invitation is scrutinized for its possible controversy quotient, its security risk.

If she were not the Queen's cousin, she would, like so many upper class women of her generation, be known outside her own circle simply as the wife of the Hon. Angus Ogilvy – and he in turn would be free to fight his case when he was involved in the Lonrho drama instead of quietly resigning. Who can blame him, if occasionally, on minor issues, Mr Ogilvy puts his foot down?

'No darling, you can't have it,' he said, as Princess Alexandra gazed rapt at a weirdly monstrous art figure, 'Florida Shopper', with piggy eyes and lurid clothes which lurked ominously lifesize in a corner of the Tate Gallery. The Princess climbed over the guarding rope to get an even closer look. 'I *meet* people like that,' she said, as if delighted that the breed had been identified.

The visit to the Tate was a private outing slotted into a busy day so they could look at the Wilson exhibition. Mr Ogilvy is a director of Sotheby's the art dealers. The gallery was still officially open to the public but funnily enough nobody else happened to be looking round the Wilson exhibition at the same time except for Alan Bowness, the director, and Lord Hutchinson, the Chairman, and his wife, who were lucky enough to be invited to dinner by Princess Alexandra: 'Oh, we'd absolutely love to,' you could hear them purring at twenty paces.

There was a faint whiff of emulsion because the Tate were busy finishing their new snack bar. Sergeant Andrew Crighton, the Princess's security man, sniffed the air – 'a bit suspicious. New paint in an art gallery.' A joke. By a security man. What next? It turns out that security men are matched to their royal charges with infinite care. Chief Inspector John Kirchin, who has been controlling the Princess's security for nine years, told me later one of the key reasons he landed the job was that he has two children exactly the same ages as young Marina and James, the Princess's children.

Earlier that afternoon the Princess had opened an independent school for dyslexic children in Princess Gate, SW7, where the fees for specialist teaching are £3,000 a year. Such well-heeled parents and their committee formed an articulate confident gathering – yet still avid with mystic wonder for the everyday acts of Royalty. The principal, Mrs Daphne Hamilton-Fairley, had met the Princess a week before at another function. 'Do you know she remembered she was coming here and she said, "I won't have to wear a hat, will I?" just like you or I would.'

Indeed the Princess did not wear a hat. Her newly blonde hair had been coiled like

Princess Alexandra takes a mother's keen interest in the latest developments in helping dyslexic children at the new Fairley School in Knightsbridge, London, a specialist establishment for children with reading difficulties. Her only current problem with her own children is to coax her son James to cram for his A levels. She has told friends she is set on dissuading him from his original ambition to be yet another royal photographer.

spun sugar that morning by Michael at Michaeljohn. She was wearing an Air Force blue crêpe coat which swung elegantly from narrow shoulders, trimmed at the neck and cuffs with toning fur, a beautiful garment which could only be worn successfully by a Royal or an actress.

She moved round the school meticulously speaking to every child. She was good with the children but clearly more at ease with their teachers. 'What will you do when we leave this room?' she asked one. And she was even better with the ladies lined up beside the buffet: 'Who's been doing all the cooking?' she asked with her most conspiratorial grin.

The magic of royalty is catching – I find I have solemnly written in my notebook the riveting fact that the Princess can cook such things as scrambled eggs but her main culinary activity is to discuss meals with her cook.

She was accompanied at the school by her full-time lady-in-waiting, Lady Mary Fitzalan Howard who is gentle and friendly and behaves slightly like a favoured secretary. You have to study Debrett to discover that she is the daughter of the late Duke of Norfolk, the one who sold Littlehampton.

The Princess and Mr Ogilvy gave each other tactful hints about lingering. 'Darling, we're stopping all their work,' he said. 'We've interrupted you thoroughly,' she said as he pored over a particularly interesting looking piece of equipment. At the reception the Princess drank a cup of black tea and ate nothing. Like most royals she never drinks alcohol and hardly eats when working. This is not mass anorexia but the effect of adrenalin. The Royal Family may be accustomed to making appearances in the same way that Lord Olivier is accustomed to going on stage – but we expect *him* to have stage fright every night so why not them?

She left the school, smiling farewells as if being pulled away quite against her will. She was driven to her suite of offices at St James's Palace and got on with some paper work with her secretary Miss Mona Mitchell. Last year her offices were infested with dry rot so her staff are currently housed in a small flat in the palace which happened to be vacant – which she herself apparently regards as vaguely shabby. She suggested that I should be received for a briefing somewhere else rather than have an outsider see the faded Osborne & Little trellis wallpaper, the ladylike mahogany desks jammed against metal filing cabinets. Outside there is the clashing male roar of the changing of the guard as one of her staff explains that the Princess worries when the secretarial staff overwork. 'She thinks it reflects on her if people see the lights on after seven.'

The Princess and Mr Ogilvy left the Tate shortly after six – that gave her less than two hours to get herself together, relaxed, refreshed and changed into a tiara and blue Bellville Sassoon evening gown for one of the most taxing evenings in the Royal Family's diary, the Diplomatic Reception. It was nearly 1 am before they got back to

Thatched House Lodge, the rambling house in Richmond Park which they bought for £150,000 when they married eighteen years ago. (The mortgage repayments are said to be in the region of £17,000 a year.)

The next morning there was scant chance of a lie-in – she had to hare back to Michaeljohn's, this time clutching her violet suede Jean Muir hat so that he could fix her hair to sweep prettily round its brim.

She arrived at the World Travel Fair

Mystery at the Tate. The Princess and her husband, the Hon. Angus Ogilvy, ponder the truth of a vast landscape at the Wilson exhibition which mysteriously depicts both Windsor and Richmond. In profile the Ogilvys, like many happily married couples, look curiously alike – both are bone thin with Grecian noses and have a propensity for quizzical smiles. The Princess's Greek nose is the genuine article. Her mother, Princess Marina, was a member of the Greek royal family. The Princess feels strongly about her heritage and close observers noted her keen interest in visiting the Greek stand at Olympia the next day.

bright and glamorous and looking as if it were all great fun. Fun? Well, a shivery blonde got up like a Page Three Boadicea paraded in front of her, plus the odd Mountie who had possibly eaten far too much quiche, while a gang of chaps in striped jackets bobbed about showing how they couldn't play jazz very well. However well intentioned, the display looked sadly silly. The Princess smiled nicely at each and every person in the tableau. Mr Ogilvy, wearing a wonderful double-breasted suit with turn-ups, looked occasionally slightly embarrassed. They both listened with attentive politeness as Lord Boyd Carpenter made possibly one of the most boring speeches anyone has ever heard – his best *bon mot*, which he underlined heavily, was that the Princess and her husband were Expert Travellers. Undaunted she set off at her jolly gallop round the stands, managing to look suitably overcome with gratitude at every freebie proffered from a small milk jug to a tin of Berlin ginger bread. 'Be nice with the coffee,' said the jokey security man as gifts were handed from the lady-in-waiting (not Lady Mary today but her part-time stand-in Lady Nicholas Gordon Lennox) to exhibition officials to carry.

A man from the Italian stand was told twice, three times, that no way was his country's exhibit on the Princess's schedule. At his fourth approach somebody made the mistake of saying 'Well where are you then?' 'Just down here,' he cried, so the Princess grinned, acknowledging his determination, and turned in the direction he beckoned. 'Just down here' turned out to be miles away, past the Bulgarians knocking themselves out in a folk dance, past some hype from the Marquess of Hertford, with an occasional further sighting of the skimpy Boadicea. The procession finally came to rest at the Italian stand where a tenor in a white frock was belting out *O Sole Mio* and our tenacious friend, not content with just her presence, now wanted her to drink coffee with him. The girl standing by his machine looked stunned. 'Espresso' he said to her. '*Coffee*' he supplemented desperately. Finally, just as the Princess was about to dart away, a scalding cup was placed in her hands. The man beamed, waiting for his praise.

'Lovely,' she smiled politely as the brew must have burnt holes in her tongue. 'Now we must go and find the Greek stand mustn't we?' she said.

That afternoon she went to see one of her dressmakers – her favourites include Maureen Baker as well as Jean Muir and Bellville Sassoon. Apparently she always goes to them rather than has sketches sent round to her. In the evening she and Mr Ogilvy and Chief Inspector Kirchin went to a private dinner-dance in Regent's Park, a jolly occasion which gave her the latest night of her week – it was well after two before they got home.

Not that the chief inspector would let slip such a revealing nugget of real information. He reiterates three times a day to whoever's listening that the Princess is 'a very private person'. To make sure she maintains her privacy he has practised to

The anonymous clamped face of a security man, curiously every bit as recognizable in plain clothes as in uniform, is a vital prop of every public appearance. The World Travel Fair at Olympia, was a mêlée of uncheckable crowds and the security team was painfully aware that the Princess in her striking violet suede matching hat and coat would have been an easy target for a warped mind. As one dectective said 'Our presence makes sure that any loony knows he would be on a kamikaze trip. He might get her but there is no doubt that we'd get him.' The guards (left) are strictly ceremonial, trumpeting a fanfare during the opening ceremony.

perfection the art of sliding away from questions however harmless and banal. 'Let's see,' he said, apparently chummy, 'Where was the dinner-dance? Can't quite remember.' Like all her staff and her 'regulars', the people she visits fairly frequently, he overtly admires her. The words 'wonderful, human, worth her weight in gold' begin to echo in your ears with almost predictable regularity.

On Thursday afternoon she went to Lancaster University of which she has been Chancellor since its inception in 1964. She visits at least twice a year, usually for two or three days at a time, although this was the first occasion she had actually spent the night on campus. Her first engagement was to listen to a celebrity lecture which was peppered much less brightly than promised with aphorisms and seemed like a long hour. She was dressed perfectly for the draughty corridors in a long skirt, velvet blouse and elegant wool cowl.

The campus is more like a new town than a university, covering 250 acres and built of yellow brick round a traffic-free shopping precinct complete with launderette and supermarket. There was a dinner after the lecture for honorary graduates attended mainly by the staff of the university. This is not Malcolm Bradbury territory and there is an almost tangible ex-pat feel about the gathering, marooned amid their modern, wonderful facilities, three miles out of Lancaster and much farther than that from the original sources of their disciplines.

The Princess has made it her business to get to know everybody on the staff, with whom she is immensely popular. The next morning when she opened a new social centre converted from an old sugar mill she chatted easily to students. She is quite keen on reminding them how the campus was little more than a perilous building site back in 1964 when it started. In earlier years there was real unrest at Lancaster but the mood is calm now if not sleepy: most students aspire to be either accountants or teachers, or so they say when they receive their degrees from the Princess.

The degree ceremonies are a challenge. There is an impressive procession with academics in full rig and a porter dressed

Not even the pomp of a Chancellor's hat and gown can dim Princess Alexandra's sparkle. As long ago as 1959 when she was officially visiting Australia she sparkled her way out of a contretemps with another hat – not her own that time but the silk top hat of the Governor of Australia. She sat on it in a limousine. Undaunted, she held the squashed topper up for all to see crying 'Look what I've done now!' Here in Lancaster more dignity prevails as she confers an honorary degree on Professor Kenneth Boulding who the previous evening had given the last of a series of memorial lectures. Serious collectors of royal minutiae should note (above) that the Princess wore the same pearl and diamond earrings day in day out this week. Centre above: Since she became Chancellor in 1965 her unstinting efforts for the University have earned the admiration of the staff. Right: When the Princess was the same age as this little girl her avowed ambition was to be a bare-backed rider in a circus – a dream destined to be forever unfulfilled.

up as a beadle with fanfares by police trumpeters. For three whole days every summer and this one afternoon in the winter the Princess hands out degrees, managing somehow to greet each student wheeling up to her with surprise and delight.

In many ways she must be the best royal any organization could hope for. She looks like a star. At forty-five she is possibly more beautiful than she has ever been, very thin, spectacularly well dressed and confident. She laughs nearly all the time, meeting people's eyes as if the occasion was a huge treat just this side of a joke. She is famous for her good temper. 'Even when she has to tell me I've done something wrong she is never unpleasant,' said Miss Mitchell at her office. Not a breath of scandal has clouded her name beyond her husband's former connection with Lonrho – which he severed rather than embarrass her. She has mastered the art of talking briefly to hundreds of people without revealing a syllable about her own life – no references even to My son, My daughter. She is said to be the Royal Family's own favourite – as evidenced by Prince Charles choosing her to be his son's godmother, though her own best friends within the family are said to be her brothers.

The only snag inherent in having this elegant and jolly princess as your VIP is that you stand scant chance of anybody else hearing about it. Barely a paragraph got into the national press about her efforts this week. But news travels other ways. A lady on the London train late on Friday afternoon was telling everybody within earshot ... 'And then Princess Alexandra said to her chauffeur, "do turn the engine off, you're churning mud over this lady's boots...".'

Pauline Peters

PRINCE AND PRINCESS MICHAEL OF KENT

Sunday

Princess: *Standard* Film Awards, Inn on The Park, London.

Monday

Prince: installation as Provincial Grand Master, Freemasons' Hall; lunch afterwards at the Connaught Rooms.

Tuesday

Early morning ride out of Knightsbridge Barracks. **Princess:** shopping for textiles, followed by research at London Library for book project.

Wednesday

Princess: 30th British–American Ball at Grosvenor House Hotel, London.

Thursday

Prince: working day in the City.
Princess: Victoria and Albert Museum Advisory Committee meeting.
Both: Dinner and violin recital at Italian Embassy.

Friday

Prince: Donington Park Race Track to test John Player Lotus Formula 1 car.
Both: to Nether Lypiatt Manor for weekend.

Princess Michael's official week began on Sunday night at the *Standard* Film Awards, in the Inn On The Park. It was one of those glittering dos where everybody cranes their neck to see who else is there. Most of them, however, were craning to get a look at the Princess, a woman of such extraordinary beauty that she outshone the assembled stars. Six feet tall, her shoulders bare, masses of blonde hair scooped up on top of her head, she towered above the small, distinguished men who were her hosts. As Jean Rook put it: 'She rises above it all, like Everest with the sun on it, and you can get a good gape at her.'

Another of her qualities is that she seemed to be actually enjoying herself. In fact, by official standards this was a particularly jolly evening, with a lot of show-biz bonhomie and clips of the winning films. The Polish-directed *Moonlighting* won the Best Film Award and the Princess presented the prize. 'Everyone else has a very real reason for being here,' she apologized. 'Perhaps I was asked because I've a Polish step-father, so I can pronounce the winner correctly.'

Later she told me: 'I didn't know I had to make a speech!' Recently she'd had to give a speech at the Woman of the Year lunch. 'I worked on it for hours – I didn't want to read it, I wanted to memorize it. Here am I, I thought, the Thinking Princess. It was being filmed for TV. So I did it, and finished, with that hot flush of achievement. It was only then that they told me the TV microphones had been broken all the time. Pride comes before a fall!'

Official functions are carefully planned in advance. Royalty, of course, always arrives last and leaves first. There's a timetable, with details of bouquets, what door to arrive at, who exactly is going to be there and who presented. This is vetted by the staff at Kensington Palace. It's here that Prince and Princess Michael of Kent, by Royal standards, keep an extremely modest household – an eight-bedroomed house with nursery – above the staff offices, called 'a doll's house' by Princess Margaret before she moved out.

This is because, unlike the other Royals, they are not on the Civil List. (The Prince didn't forfeit this by marrying the divorced, Catholic Marie Christine von Reibnitz, though he did forfeit his right to succession to the Throne.) Having no public money they are obliged, as the Princess once said, 'to sing for our supper'. They pay no rent at Kensington Palace, but they have to pay rates, bills and wages.

They are, in fact, a working couple and have to juggle official functions, for which they're not paid, with their professional commitments. Unlike the rest of the Royal Family they have to ask: How far is it? Can we afford the time and the travel? However, in 1981 this didn't stop them from attending 120 official functions – 19 more than Princess Margaret. They're much in demand, being stunningly glamorous, as well as both spirited and amenable. 'Last time she came she was hugely pregnant,' says a hostess. 'And, you know, she attended a charity auction just seven days after she had her second baby.'

On Monday, at 10.30 am, the Prince was installed into something secret and

The Princess joins a cluster of celebrities including Jane Asher, Robert Morley, Trevor Howard and Felicity Kendal at the *Standard* Film Awards at the Inn on the Park Hotel, London. Felicity Kendal presented the Best Actress award to her sister Jennifer for her role in *36 Chowringhee Lane* and the Princess presented the Best Film prize for the Polish-directed *Moonlighting*. She joked that she had been asked because she had a Polish stepfather and could pronounce director Jerzy Skolimowski's name correctly.

Princess Michael choosing fabrics to cover a four-poster bed, at Claremont Fabrics, in Carnaby Street, with the help of Claremont partner Richard Jeffree. The Princess studied for two years at the Victoria and Albert Museum and specializes in the restoration of 18th-century houses. She started her own interior design business, Szapar Designs, before her marriage to Prince Michael and still runs it, though on an occasional basis. She oversaw the interior decoration of their own country house, Nether Lypiatt, where innovations include a hand-stencilled hall and stairwell.

Returning books (far right) to the London Library, the distinguished lending library where a year's subscription is £60. Princess Michael is writing a biography of Elizabeth Stuart, the 17th-century Queen of Bohemia and daughter of James I, who was known as the 'Queen of Hearts'. She tries to set aside two and a half hours each day after lunch for her writing.

Masonic at the Freemasons' Hall. On Tuesday morning at 8.30 am the Royal couple were mounted on horseback and clattering out of Knightsbridge Barracks. They often go for an early-morning ride; while the Prince is passionate about cars, the Princess is a keen horse-woman, hunts in Gloucestershire, and has learned how to ride side-saddle. Cantering through the mist, the bearded Prince looked uncannily like his grandfather King George V.

On Tuesday the Princess went to Claremont Fabrics, a cavernous basement near Carnaby Street. Before her marriage the Princess studied Art History in Vienna, interior design in London, and studied for two years at the Victoria and Albert Museum; she then became an interior designer with her own firm, Szapar Designs, and still continues this from her home at Nether Lypiatt. She specializes in the restoration of 18th-century houses, and at Claremont she was choosing fabrics for a four-poster bed, and complementary wall-coverings.

'Isn't it like a souk!' she said, as the fabrics were spread, billowing, around her. 'I love muddy colours,' she said, 'that look as if they've been there for years. You can stain fabric with tea. My mother-in-law poured milk all over her Persian carpets to bleach out the colours, it was the fashion then.' 'In fact, it's the least glamorous job in the world,' she laughed, and discreetly asked the manager the price.

Then a dash through the clogged streets of the West End to the London Library, to return some research books. Often she drives herself, in an Escort, but today the security man/driver was behind the wheel of the dark-green Daimler with its crest on the bonnet. Her other job at the moment is writing a biography of Elizabeth Stuart, the Queen of Bohemia. 'I try to work each afternoon, from 2.30 to 5.'

On Wednesday evening the Princess attended the 30th British-American Ball at Grosvenor House. On these official occasions her acting lady-in-waiting, Miss 'Jumbo' Frost, accompanies her. This was a huge affair, with dinner and a long cabaret of Gurkha soldiers performing an Off-To-The-Falklands dance; some of the men were dressed in saris, playing the sorrowing wives. It was half moving, half terribly boring. And then there was dancing afterwards to a band of middle-aged swingers in black open-necked shirts and medallions.

On these occasions the Royal representative has to look interested throughout, being on display to 1,200 people. 'There's a lot of homework to be done,' says a member of their staff. 'They're not just sitting there; they're with the hosts, they have to know all about the organization. They're with the people whose life is that subject.' Then there are the presentations,

for which they must be prepared with all the biographical details. And last but not least there's the public. 'They've paid good money to come; you can't tuck Royalty away into VIP lounges; you have to give the public their money's worth. Our job is to liaise, to stage-manage these functions so that everyone is satisfied.'

The next morning, Thursday, the Prince went to work at Aitken Hume, a high-gloss investment and banking group launched by the Prince's fellow Old Etonian Jonathan Aitken and his cousin Timothy. The Prince joined in 1982, having previously been in

the Army and in military intelligence. He is the first member of the Royal Family to work in the City. He goes into the office two days a week and, for his non-executive role, is paid between £5,000 and £10,000 a year. 'Today he's working on his personal investments,' said Timothy Aitken, 'and those of some of our clients. Now that he knows the language, we're hoping he'll be working three full days a week for us.'

What do the other employees call him? 'Sir.' His other paid directorship is with STC. There, apparently, the Prince was once accosted in the lobby by an American

executive shouting: 'Great to meet you, Mike baby!' Well, he was American.

While her husband was at work, the Princess went to the Victoria and Albert for one of the two-monthly meetings of the Advisory Committee, of which she is a member. This is a sign of the esteem in which she is held by the applied arts world as there are just twenty members and they run the museum. Carrying her briefcase, she walked through the galleries, attracting the awed gaze of anoraked tourists. 'Don't you love this place!' she said. 'It smells like home!' She pointed out objects en route –

Arriving at the Grosvenor House Hotel for the £25-a-head British-American Ball, Princess Michael meets the Canadian High Commissioner Jean Wadds (left). The British-American Associates were founded in 1931 to work for better understanding between the peoples of Britain, Canada and the United States. Current Presidents of the organization include former British ambassadors to Washington Sir Nicholas Henderson, and Peter Jay – seen later in the evening (far left) dancing with the Princess, who wore a primrose yellow off-the-shoulder ball gown trimmed with ostrich feathers.

Lord Mottistone, a President of British-American Associates, rises to speak at their 30th annual ball where the Princess is guest of honour. Not being on the Civil List means, the Princess once said, that she and her husband have to sing for their supper.

A normal working day for Prince Michael at Aitken Hume, a banking and investment group launched in 1981 which he joined a year later. The first Royal by birth to work in the City, he puts in two days a week, working either on the chic, open plan floor where the Stock Exchange prices flicker on a TV screen, or in his own private office a floor above with other directors who include Jonathan Aitken. The Prince has another paid directorship with Standard Telephones and Cables which he took up in 1981 after leaving the Army.

European bronzes and sculptures. She has no trace of an Austrian accent; the only reminder of her origin is the fact that she can pronounce the names of foreign artists properly.

She paused to admire the enormous Great Bed of Ware. 'Our bed's not quite as big as this, but then we do have five cats sleeping with us. The Burmese is always catching animals and dragging them in under the bed. You hear these cracking noises; my husband says, "Do we have to sleep on top of an abattoir?".'

She is a great cat-lover and takes the two pedigree ones – the Burmese and a Siamese which she suspects may be gay – down to the country each weekend in her car. 'I'm thinking of entering the Burmese for the 'Most Majestic Moggie' competition in the *Tatler*. I'm too mean to buy magazines but I heard about this.' The other three cats are ordinary mouse-catchers – 'except they never catch anything'.

That evening, Thursday, there was a private function at the Italian Embassy where both the Prince and the Princess listened to the soloist Salvatore Accardo, with dinner afterwards. Then on Friday morning Prince Michael went up to Donington Park Race Track, in the Midlands. 'If his driver's driving,' said the organizers, 'he'll be here in three hours. If he's driving, in

In the English Sculpture Gallery of the Victoria and Albert Museum, Princess Michael pauses to talk to Stephen Calloway, assistant to the Museum's director Sir Roy Strong, before a meeting of the Museum's advisory council. The council meets every two months, and fellow members include Jean Muir and Sir Terence Conran. Topic of the day was the future governing system of the Museum, which is to become a trustee museum and be taken out of the civil service administration.

Prince Michael is fascinated by everything mechanical and learnt to drive on private roads long before he was old enough to drive on public thoroughfares. He competed in the 1970 World Cup Rally from London to Mexico, is President of the RAC, the Motor Industry Research Association and the Institute of the Motor Industry. Here he is putting a Lotus Formula 1 racing car through its paces at Donington Park. He had seen the car at the Motor Show, expressed an interest and an invitation from Lotus followed. It was the first time he had driven a Formula 1 car.

two.' Prince Michael is a speed fanatic, an ex-British Bobsleigh Champion and rally driver; in 1970 he competed in the World Cup Rally from London to Mexico, and is respected in the motor-racing world as a fellow professional. He is also heavily involved in the motor industry; among other posts he is President of the RAC.

The Donington Park occasion was a private invitation to try out the John Player Lotus Formula 1 racing car. It was a friendly, low key affair - no reporters, no spectators. Even so, the mechanics were looking remarkably spruce and, before he arrived, it was gently suggested to one that he change his blue plimsolls for something in black. In fact, fifteen of us were watching the Prince's every move as he emerged in crimson padded overalls and climbed into the racing car. And he was off.

Soon he was zooming past the pits at 140 mph. With awe, we gazed at the lap chart. 'You wouldn't believe this is his first time in a Formula 1,' said a mechanic. 'At this rate I'll be out of a job,' smiled Nigel Mansell, one of the two top drivers in the Lotus Team. 'If we had him with us,' he sighed, 'just think of the sponsorship.' After many laps the tyres needed changing and it took three attempted pit stops to get the Prince to slow down and come in. 'He really is a racing driver!' they laughed. 'They all do that.' The Prince took off his helmet. 'Absolutely sensational!' he smiled.

And then it was straight off to the country for the weekend. Their country house is in the heart of increasingly Royal Gloucestershire, with Prince Charles's house and Princess Anne's nearby. Nether Lyppiatt Manor which they bought in 1981 for

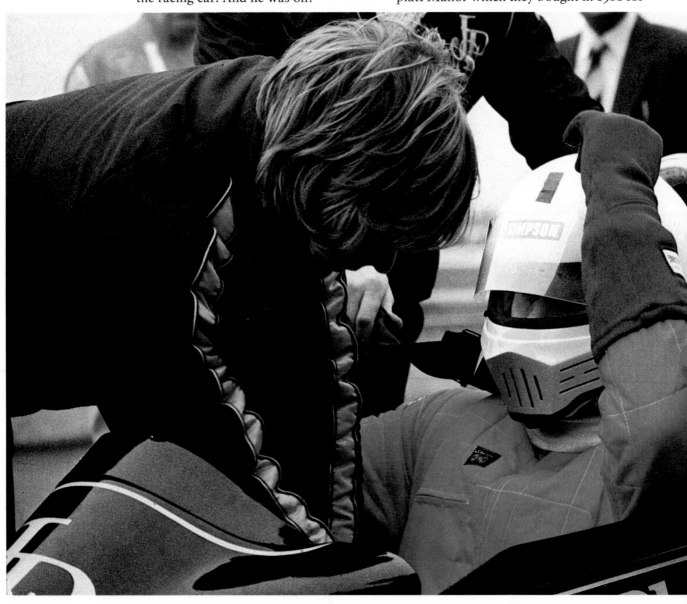

£300,000 has been called 'the most beautiful small house in Britain'; is reputedly haunted, has twelve bedrooms, eight bathrooms and a heated swimming-pool (surprisingly enough, there is no pool at Kensington Palace). Here they can relax with their guests and their two small children. They eat and drink sparingly; they are vehemently anti-smoking.

To the world at large the Prince is the shyer of the two, and more difficult to know. The Princess is more high-profile; she's a full-blooded woman who delights in attention. One newspaper described her as possessing 'limitless social ambition and the energy of a Lippizaner mare'. Says one of their staff: 'I've been offered three times the amount for another job but I wouldn't go, they're a smashing couple.'

Deborah Moggach

In go the royal earplugs as Prince Michael readies himself for his Formula 1 test drive at Donington. He is a speed fanatic and, like so many members of the Royal Family, is drawn to scary sports. He took part in the 1969 newspaper-sponsored transatlantic air race and won the British Bobsleigh Championships at St Moritz in 1972 (he retired from that sport in 1974). His cars include a Rolls Royce, a Daimler, a souped-up Ford Escort XR 3 (the Princess has an XR 2) and a Range Rover.

THE YOUNG ROYALS

The youngest of the young royals: the latest additions to the Windsor dynasty, Prince William (born 21 June 1982) and Princess Anne's daughter Zara (born in May the year before), are wheeled through the tranquil grounds of the Balmoral estate by their respective nannies, Barbara Barnes and Pat Moss.

The young William faces the camera (inset) with some doubt as he is shown off by his mother, Princess Diana, at an informal session at Highgrove, the Gloucestershire home of the Prince and Princess of Wales. When plans for the couple's Spring 1983 tour of Australia and New Zealand were announced a new royal precedent was set – the baby was to go with them instead of, as in the past, staying at home.

When he was young and closely protected from public gaze, the Palace staff nicknamed him Andy Pandy. And when he was sixteen and exposed to the sort of press coverage he can expect for the rest of his life, the headline writers dubbed him Randy Andy, a name he hates but which has stuck in the seven years since. Prince Andrew is undoubtedly the brightest star among a great clutch of 'new' royalty – there are sixteen of them, some scarcely known to the public – waiting to share between them to a greater or lesser extent, the royal round of duty.

At twenty-three, a serving naval officer and veteran of the Falklands campaign, Andrew has not only experienced the realities of war, but he has also shared, with Princess Diana, some of the less welcome media attention that is part of today's royal inheritance – and coped with it rather better than his younger brother who last year loosed a gunshot over the heads of waiting pressmen at Sandringham whose curiosity he found suddenly unbearable.

Andrew, a practical joker who by repute once put a whoopee cushion on the Queen Mother's chair and when younger tried to tie the boot laces of a Buckingham Palace sentry together ('Andrew was not always a little ray of sunshine,' said the Queen) was deliberately kept out of the limelight as a child, as was his brother Edward. Because of his parents' decision to try to shield his childhood from publicity, Andrew, the first child to be born to a reigning monarch in over a hundred years, was the subject of a rash of distressing rumours

that he might be in some way handicapped. His first schooling was at Buckingham Palace and at eight he went to Heatherdown prep school followed by Gordonstoun – with a six month spell at Canada's Lakefield College in 1977.

At Gordonstoun he became cricket captain like his father before him, played first team hockey and got three A level exam passes in history, English and economics and political studies. He entered the Britannia Royal Naval College, Dartmouth, having signed up for a twelve year engagement with the Royal Navy, in September 1979.

Now a senior helicopter pilot with 820 Squadron based at the Royal Naval air station Culdrose, Andrew, who as second son to the Queen will one day become the Duke of York, has undertaken few public duties. (He scored one mention in the Court Circular in 1981 when he made a speech after a rugby match at Twickenham. It went down rather well.) But his lifestyle does reflect exactly who he is. He started the week of our study on a three day pass from his squadron, shooting wild pig in Liechtenstein as a guest of Prince Franz Josef II, an old family friend. And he spent the next weekend with the Queen and Prince Philip pheasant shooting at the home of Lord Brabourne before his next naval assignment, a three day course in military intelligence with the Army Intelligence Corps at Ashford in Kent.

Prince Andrew is also not exactly hardup – he earns over £9,000 from the Navy and, since his eighteenth birthday, has a Civil List payment of £20,000, most of which is invested on his behalf by the Royal

Prince Andrew at the controls of a naval Lynx helicopter. He learned to fly at RAF Benson, the home of the Queen's Flight, when he was nineteen, five months before joining the Navy. He has dashing good looks (earning him, whether he might like it or not, a place alongside Mick Jagger in the International Bachelor Women's Society 1983 top ten chart of the world's single men) and a vital sense of humour.

Princess Margaret's two children, Viscount Linley and Lady Sarah Armstrong-Jones, relax with Prince Charles (above right) during a polo match at Windsor Great Park. Eighteen-year-old Lady Sarah went to Bedales school like her brother and has taken a not dissimilar direction to him towards a career, studying at the Camberwell School of Art in London.

Prince Edward the teacher, quieter than the extrovert Andrew, in action (right) in a Wanganui Collegiate, New Zealand, classroom. At the end of his first term there he told an interviewer: 'There are times when it can be good fun. There are times when it's sheer hell. I enjoy the challenge.'

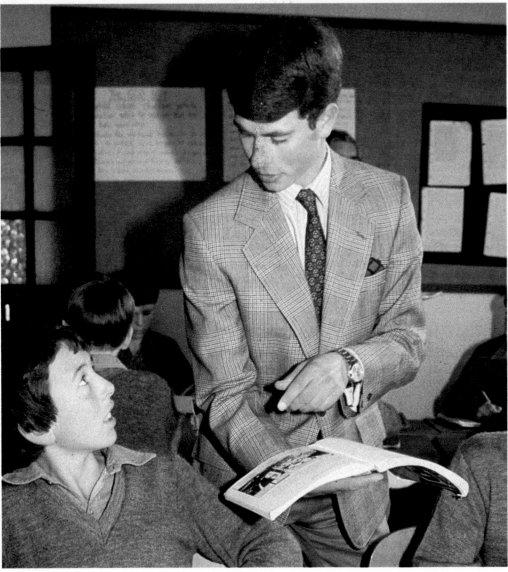

Trustees (the Prime Minister, the Chancellor of the Exchequer and the Keeper of the Privy Purse). His only official home is a suite of three rooms in Buckingham Palace.

Prince Edward, at nineteen years old, gets a Civil List entitlement £16,183. He is currently in his second term as a junior house tutor at Wanganui Collegiate, New Zealand's leading boarding school, where he lives in Selwyn House (in quarters described as 'cramped' – a special building had to be built alongside to accommodate his bodyguard). He teaches some history and English, helps out with sports and hobbies. In December he flew, as a guest of the New Zealand Government, for a week's tour of the Antarctic, visiting scientific stations, the American bases at the South Pole and McMurdo Sound and the huts on Ross Island once used by Scott and Shackleton. Wanganui headmaster Ian McKinnon reported that the young Prince did tremendously well in his first term, impressing the school with his vitality and wide-ranging outlook. Edward, quieter than the extrovert Andrew, likes birdwatching and fly-fishing.

Edward started his early schooling at Buckingham Palace with James Ogilvy, Princess Alexandra's son, Lady Helen Windsor, the Duke of Kent's daughter, and Lady Sarah Armstrong-Jones, Princess Margaret's daughter. (All four of them were born in 1964, the first time in over 150 years that so many young royals had been born within one year.) He then went to Gibbs School, on to Heatherdown and then Gordonstoun where he became head boy and gained nine O level and three A level passes (hence one nickname: Educated Eddie. He has also been tagged Steady Eddie, and latterly, by Princess Diana, Scooter, after the Muppet.)

He returns from New Zealand to go up to Jesus College, Cambridge, a matter of some public debate because of his poor A level grades, though a protest petition

Viscount Linley (left) pictured at his work bench in the co-operative that he and his three friends have set up in an old bakery, in Dorking, Surrey. He makes furniture by hand and doesn't think his name helps sell his wares.

Peter and Zara Phillips (above), pictured in the nursery at their parents' Gloucestershire home, Gatcombe. Peter is five, Zara nearly two. Princess Anne is a devoted mother, determined her children should not be spoilt.

organized by a couple of undergraduates failed to gain wide support. Prince Edward has also completed the rather tough Royal Marine Selection course and is expected to begin officer training after Cambridge.

As the Order of Succession (see page 6) shows, there is an ample supply of royal talent to inherit the duties of their parents. However, there are already more active members of the Royal Family than at any time in recent history and most of those can count on many more productive years ahead. The dilemma for the young Royals as they enter adulthood is how to fit into a modern society that will not tolerate kindly an aimless grace and favour sort of life, without forgoing the values and lifestyle we have come to expect of them. They are mostly also too young to have decided, or to have had decided for them, whether or not to join the 'business' side of being royal.

Typical is Viscount Linley, twenty-one-year-old son of Princess Margaret and ninth in line to the throne. Educated at Gibbs School, Ashdown House Prep school at Forest Row, Sussex, and then Millbrook School, Berkshire, before failing to gain entry into his father's old school, Eton, he received his later education at the progressive coed Bedales. After Bedales he took a two years' craftsman's course in carpentry at Parnham House, Dorset.

Now he has set up a co-operative workshop venture in Dorking, Surrey, with three friends and runs his own business as plain David Linley, Furniture Maker. He drives a second-hand blue MGB which he rebuilt himself, and cycles around Dorking where he shares a rented house with fellow co-operative worker Charlie Wheeler-Carmical, an architect's son.

David Linley doesn't use his title while working, does not get asked to fulfil public duties (yet) and nor does he aspire to (yet), although he does pop up publicly now and then escorting his mother. Princess Margaret's often quoted remark, 'My children are not royal, they just happen to have an aunt who is Queen', is not only being borne out in practice, but it may have a wider relevance among the burgeoning clan of royal cousins.

Stephen Clackson

Marina and James Ogilvy. She is sixteen years old and at boarding school at St Mary's, Wantage. A keen pianist, she once danced in a children's ballet at the Theatre Royal, Drury Lane. James is eighteen and has left his father's old school, Eton, where he passed thirteen O level exams and three A's. He is studying to improve his A level grades and hopes to get into Oxford.

Alexander, the Earl of Ulster, and his sister Lady Davina Windsor, two of the Duke and Duchess of Gloucestershire's children, leave Barnwell parish church hand-in-hand after the christening of their younger sister, Lady Rose.

Lady Helen Windsor, eighteen, daughter of the Duke and Duchess of Kent, lives with friends in London whilst studying to improve her A level grades. Originally at St Mary's, Wantage, she went on to Gordonstoun at sixteen.

Lord Frederick Windsor who is now three years old. He has a younger sister, Lady Gabriella Windsor, who is known as Ella. The children have a Canadian nanny, Jean Rowcliffe.

Lord Nicholas Windsor (left) who, at eleven, is the youngest of the Duke and Duchess of Kent's three children. Lady Helen Windsor (see above) is his sister and George, the Earl of St Andrews, his elder brother who was the first member of the Royal Family to become a King's Scholar at Eton (an academic award which saves the £6,000-plus-a-year fees). The nineteen-year-old Earl, known to his friends as Stan, is now at Downing College Cambridge, reading history.

THE ROYAL COURTIERS

Wherever she goes, the Queen is surrounded by seldom seen men and women who ensure that the wheels of her life run smoothly. The Royal Household is huge and many of its ancient titles and positions are held by various aristocrats who have little to do in practice. But there is a top-flight team of key full-time Palace employees who consult the Queen daily about her life and work. Here she is escorted to the polo field at Windsor by one of them, Lieutenant-Colonel Sir John Miller. As Crown Equerry, Sir John is responsible for 'cars, coaches and horses', as well as the nine gardeners, hundred maintenance staff, dozen chauffeurs and forty grooms and coachmen employed at Buckingham Palace alone. Top man in the inner circle is the Queen's private secretary, Sir Philip Moore (inset left), the most powerful person in the Palace apart from the monarch herself. Her senior lady-in-waiting is the Mistress of the Robes, at present the Duchess of Grafton (inset centre), whose team of eight includes Lady Susan Hussey (inset right), a particular favourite in Royal circles, and godmother to Prince William of Wales.

Prince Philip's official biographer, Basil Boothroyd, was walking out of Buckingham Palace one day when he bumped into the Queen's then private secretary, Sir Michael Adeane. As they passed the time of day, Adeane patiently answering a couple of points that were on the writer's mind, Boothroyd got the faint impression that he was detaining the great man ever so slightly against his will. It was another couple of minutes, however, before Adeane excused himself with profuse apologies: 'I do hope you'll forgive me, but I've just heard that my house is on fire. I wouldn't mind, but as it's a part of St James's Palace ...'

The tale is a favourite among those few outsiders regularly welcomed within the Palace, catching as it does the combination of urbanity, charm and unflappability which is the mark of the senior courtier. It also has the right twang of other-worldliness about it: when you scrunch across the gravel of the Palace forecourt, wander its endless, ornate corridors in search of these distinguished, seldom seen, very formal men, you feel you are entering a giant cocoon rarely penetrated by the real world.

It's a deceptive impression. The handful of ex-diplomats, military men, businessmen and bankers who grind the mills of the royal machine are shrewd, hard-headed realists with their feet firmly on the red-carpeted ground. They have to combine the tactical skills of politicians with the utter discretion of senior civil servants. In a world where the tiniest error can have huge repercussions, they must wear an ever-watchful eye in the suave social face

they present to the world. Like all politicians, diplomats and civil servants, they can also be insufferably self-important.

The still point of this slowly turning world is the monarch's private secretary, the most powerful figure in the Palace apart from the Queen herself. Elizabeth II has had four: Sir Alan Lascelles, whom she inherited from her father for the first year of her reign; Sir Michael (now Lord) Adeane (1953-72), Sir Martin (now Lord) Charteris (1972-77), and the present incumbent, Sir Philip Moore.

Both Sir Philip's predecessors were Old Etonians, both lieutenant-colonels with distinguished service records, both excellent shots and both artists in their spare time. Like them, Moore served a Palace apprenticeship as deputy private secretary; otherwise, however, he is from a slightly different mould.

Moore's family background is much less of the 'tweedy sort' so reviled by Lord Altrincham in his famous 1957 attack on the Queen and her courtiers. (For starters, his daughter is married to Peter Gabriel, a founder-member of the Genesis pop group.) The son of a civil servant, Moore was educated at Cheltenham and Brasenose College, Oxford, where his classical studies were interrupted by wartime service in Bomber Command (he was taken prisoner in 1942). On his return to Oxford he won rugger and hockey blues, and played as an England rugby international. He also played cricket for Oxfordshire.

Moore gave up a high-flying civil service career to join the Royal Household in 1966. Principal private secretary to the First Lord of the Admiralty in 1957–58, he was British Deputy High Commissioner in Singapore from 1963 to 1965 and then chief public relations officer at the Ministry of Defence (and thus press officer to the then Secretary of State, one Denis Healey). Appointed GCVO in the last New Year honours list, Sir Philip is a slightly more extrovert character than either Adeane or Charteris. Though less of a deep-dyed conservative, he has striven more to maintain the status quo than to streamline the public face of the modern monarchy.

All that may change in three years' time, when Moore will retire at the age of sixty-five. The odds are that he will be succeeded by his deputy, Sir William Heseltine, a dynamic fifty-two-year-old Australian who joined the Royal employ as assistant press secretary in 1965. It was Heseltine who masterminded the 1969 television film *Royal Family*, which was the greatest leap forward in this or indeed any recent reign in monarchical public relations.

The Queen needed some persuading that her subjects should be allowed to peep into the private lives of her family, not merely at the Palace, but in their several other homes around the land. It would be the first time in British history that a monarch had taken such a risk with her mystique. But Bill Heseltine shrewdly talked Elizabeth II into it – and the film was, as she herself was the first to admit afterwards, an unqualified success. It is thought in Palace circles that other such innovations may mark his term of office.

These rarefied Palace heights are approached by only one other figure, Robert Fellowes, assistant private secretary to the Queen and thus No. 3 in this very exclusive hierarchy. An old Etonian and former banker, forty-one-year-old Fellowes spotted the Spencer family just before Prince Charles; he married Lady Diana's elder sister, Lady Jane, in 1978. Which makes one wonder if the private secretary to Britain's next king will be his brother-in-law.

It is a matter of daily routine, whether the court is in London or elsewhere, that one of these three men will see the Queen each morning to go over the day's schedule, brief her on the audiences ahead, collect

Least conspicuous of the royal courtiers are the Special Branch officers assigned to protect members of the Royal Family. But they can form some of the closest friendships a Royal personage will ever know. This is certainly true of Superintendent John Maclean (left), who has 'minded' Prince Charles for more than a decade.

Only a handful of senior courtiers see the Queen every day of her working life. Two of them are her deputy private secretary, Australian-born Sir William Heseltine (below), and Michael Shea (bottom), a former diplomat who is now the Queen's press secretary and a prolific novelist.

the daily boxes of state papers, and help her deal with correspondence.

Private letters she will answer herself, in her own hand, writing ER in the corner where you or I would place the stamp; they are then despatched either by messenger or by mail from the Palace post office (registered post, of course, to deter inquisitive Post Office employees). Many of the cries for help which arrive from her subjects will simply be passed to the relevant Government department; to those which strike a chord, she will dictate the outlines of a reply to her private secretary, and he will then compose one of those letters which begins 'Her Majesty has commanded me to thank you for your letter of the 12th ...'

The only other member of the Palace staff who sees the Queen on business virtually every day is her press secretary, the man responsible for handling press coverage of all Royal appearances, and for responding to the myriad demands for exclusive interviews, photo sessions, vital statistics and so on.

The Queen's present press secretary is her most popular so far (both with the Royal Family itself, and with the press), Michael Shea, a Gordonstoun-educated former diplomat who was Deputy Director of British Information Services in New York at the time of the Queen's visit to the US in 1976 and the Prince of Wales's the following year. His handling of both events so endeared him to all concerned that he was invited to succeed Ronald Allison, the TV commentator, in 1978. Shea, an engaging forty-four-year-old Scotsman, had already published five novels under the pen-name of Michael Sinclair; since leaving the FO he has been free to write under his own name, and has maintained – despite such minor distractions as royal weddings and royal babies – a prolific output.

These four men constitute the inner circle who are in day-to-day contact with the sovereign, making the decisions which dictate her daily working life. There are four other key figures, equally anonymous to the general public, who keep the wheels of the royal juggernaut in motion: the Lord Chamberlain, the Keeper of the Privy Purse, the Master of the Household and the Crown Equerry.

Most of 'the great offices of the realm', so called since the reign of Henry VIII in all public lists of the monarch's household, are now merely honorific positions entailing few duties, inherited by virtue either of political office or lofty birth. The Lord Chancellor, the Lord President of the Council and the Lord Privy Seal are all these days politicians; the Lord Great Chamberlain, the Earl Marshal, the Lord High Constable, the Lord Steward of the Household and the Master of the Horse – all roles still proudly filled by sundry aristocrats – are obliged to do little more than turn out in ceremonial uniforms on state occasions.

The office of Lord Chamberlain, however, remains a very busy and responsible one, occupied by a man of substance and distinction. The Lord Chamberlain is not merely responsible for all departments of the Royal Household, and for organizing state visits, court ceremonies (including, for instance, 1981's royal wedding) and garden parties, but for all appointments to the Household (medical, ecclesiastical, military, diplomatic) and such further-flung appointees as the Gentlemen Usher of the Sword of State, Black Rod, the Honourable Corps of Gentlemen-At-Arms, the Queen's Bodyguard of the Yeomen of the Guard (not to be confused with the Yeomen Warders of the Tower of London, alias Beefeaters) and the Queen's Bodyguard for Scotland.

All this may smack of the 'idiotic flummery' with which the late Richard Crossman lost patience in his diaries, of kissing hands and walking backwards in the monarch's presence (as new Privy Councillors and Cabinet ministers must do to this day). But the Captain of the Honourable Corps of Gentlemen-At-Arms, for instance (whose thirty-two members also include Harbinger, Standard Bearer, Clerk of the Cheque and Adjutant) also holds the not unimportant office of Chief Government Whip in the House of Lords, at present Lord Denham.

Also under the Lord Chamberlain's sway come such disparate luminaries as the Master of the Queen's Music (at present the Australian composer Malcom Williamson), the poet laureate (Sir John Betjeman), the Surveyor of the Queen's Pictures (once Sir Anthony Blunt, now Sir Oliver Millar), the Constable of Windsor Castle (Marshal of the Royal Air Force Sir John Grandy), the Keeper of the Crown Jewels in the Tower of London (Major-General G. H. Mills), the Queen's Bargemaster (Mr E. Hunt, also i-c Her Majesty's Watermen), and the Keeper of the Swans (Mr F. J. Turk), who must each year round up all the cygnets on the Thames between London Bridge and Henley, and ring the few hundred which belong to the Queen.

The office of the Lord Chamberlain – the senior member of the Royal Household – mounts a huge administrative operation. Until 1971 the post was held by Old Etonian Lord Cobbold, a former Governor of the Bank of England. He was succeeded by the present incumbent, Lord Maclean, 27th Chief of Clan Maclean, a former Scots Guard who until his appointment was Chief Scout of the Commonwealth. A close personal friend of the Queen, Maclean commutes a great deal between his suite of offices in St James's Palace and 'ops HQ' at Buckingham Palace, which houses the three other key management staff members in the Royal Household.

Any published list will tell you that John Stradling Thomas, Conservative MP for Monmouth and Deputy Chief Whip, is Treasurer of the Queen's Household, with the Hon. Anthony Berry, MP for Enfield, Southgate (and son of the newspaper baron Lord Kemsley), as Comptroller and Carol Mather, MP for Esher, as Vice-Chamberlain. But these too are purely honorific, political titles. They do have minor chores to perform but the man really in charge of the Queen's money is the Keeper of the Privy Purse, Mr Peter Miles.

Also styled Treasurer to the Queen, Mr Miles (a former banker, ex-Eton and Sandhurst) works closely with her bankers, Coutts, and her solicitors, Farrers, the Crown Estate Commissioners and the Dept of the Environment over the maintenance of those royal homes which belong to the Crown: Buckingham Palace, Windsor Castle and St James's Palace. He is also Receiver-General of the Duchy of Lancaster, and financial overseer of everything from the Queen's racing stables to the ex-

tremely valuable stamp collection amassed by George V (and recently pored over by one Michael Fagan). Responsibility for the private estates – Sandringham, Balmoral – falls to the deputy Keeper, Major Shane Blewitt (ex-Irish Guards), while the deputy treasurer to the Queen, Mr Russell Wood, administers the income from the Civil List.

The other two men primarily responsible for the nuts and bolts of Royal life are also obscured by grandees with mediaeval titles. The Lord Steward of the Household, for instance, is the Duke of Northumberland, but in practice the Duke turns out only for state banquets and other such ceremonial occasions. The 'hotel manager', as he is known to Palace colleagues, is in fact Vice-Admiral Sir Peter Ashmore, the Master of the Household. Once Chief of Allied Staff at NATO Headquarters, S. Europe, Sir Peter is now in charge of banquets and garden parties, keeping tabs on staff such as the Palace Steward, the Yeomen of the Wine Cellars, the Pages of the Backstairs and of the Presence, and of course the Palace chef.

Similarly, the nine gardeners, hundred maintenance staff, dozen chauffeurs and forty grooms and coachmen at the Palace are nominally under the sway of the Master of the Horse, the Earl of Westmorland. But in practice the man in charge of 'cars, coaches and horses' is the Crown Equerry, Lieutenant-Colonel Sir John Miller. Another Old Etonian Guards officer, holder of the DSO and the MC, Sir John is also responsible for the Queen's thirty horses, seventy odd carriages, and twenty or so cars. A keen huntsman, and one of the mentors of Prince Charles's youth, it was Sir John who persuaded the Prince of Wales to indulge his passion for hunting, despite the public (and now marital) controversy it was bound to cause.

There is one further group of people in daily contact with the Queen, purely as helpmeets and companions. These are her ladies-in-waiting, eight close friends handpicked personally by the monarch to attend her on public outings and help out at home with such chores as correspondence. They are under the command of the Mistress of the Robes, in status the female equivalent of the Lord Chamberlain, beside whom she

Private secretary to the Princess of Wales is Oliver Everett (below), a high-flying FO man and reputedly an even better polo-player than Prince Charles.

Princess Diana has a team of four ladies-in-waiting, none of them particularly close friends before her marriage. Foremost among them is Miss Anne Beckwith-Smith (bottom).

.processes on state occasions. Formerly the Dowager Duchess of Devonshire, this is now the Duchess of Grafton, whose main responsibility is to organize the rota of her eight colleagues.

The two senior of the eight, styled Ladies of the Bedchamber, are the Marchioness of Abergavenny and the Countess of Airlie, sisters-in-law respectively of the late Lord Rupert Nevill (the Duke of Edinburgh's devoted friend and private secretary) and Princess Alexandra. Then come the Women of the Bedchamber – Dame Mary Morrison, Lady Susan Hussey, Lady Abel Smith and Mrs John Dugdale – and the Extra Women of the Bedchamber, Mrs John Woodroffe and Lady Rose Baring. (Also styled an Extra Woman of the Bedchamber, but helping out on a more occasional basis since her retirement from long service in the Palace press office, is Mrs Michael Wall.)

The ladies-in-waiting receive modest remuneration for their services, which continue wherever the Queen is in residence. The usual 'tour of duty' is a fortnight at a time. In London they will stay overnight at the Palace only if a late night engagement is to be followed by an early morning one; in the Queen's other homes, however, they will lunch and dine with Her Majesty, and help look after the house guests. Their male equivalents are the equerries who dance attendance on the men of the Royal Family; these are usually shorter-term, military appointments, lacking quite the same degree of intimacy as ladies-in-waiting share with the Queen or the royal princesses they attend.

The Princess of Wales has three new friends as ladies-in-waiting, primarily Miss Anne Beckwith-Smith, assisted on occasion by the Hon. Mrs Vivian Baring and Mrs George West. She is lucky to have inherited from her husband a particularly bright, polo-playing FO man, Oliver Everett, as her private secretary. Prince Charles himself chose a barrister, Edward Adeane (son of Lord Adeane) to succeed his first private secretary, Squadron Leader Sir David Checketts, in 1979. An old Navy shipmate of the Prince's, Michael Colborne, is secretary and accountant to their household.

Each of the other Royals has a small private office to run their affairs, in each case headed by a private secretary. The recent death of Lord Rupert Nevill has left a hole at the top of the Duke of Edinburgh's staff, temporarily filled at present by Mr Richard Davies, a former director of Ferranti. The Queen Mother (who has her own Lord Chamberlain in the Earl of Dalhousie) has since 1956 enjoyed the services of Colditz veteran Sir Martin Gilliat, while Lord Mountbatten's former private secretary, John Barratt, now looks after Prince and Princess Michael of Kent. Old Etonians again abound: apart from Adeane and Gilliatt, they are represented by Princess Margaret's private secretary, Lord Napier, and the Gloucester family's Sir Simon Bland. The only Old Harrovian private secretary is the Kents', Sir Philip Hay, and the only female one Princess Alexandra's, Miss Mona Mitchell. Princess Anne and Captain Mark Phillips are served by Lieutenant Colonel Peter Gibbs.

With the office of the Queen's press secretary also looking after the Duke of Edinburgh and the Prince and Princess of Wales, the Queen Mother is the only other member of the Royal Family to have her own full-time press secretary, Major John Griffin, who has been with her since the days of the Peter Townsend affair, and has ever since helped out with Princess Margaret's press relations when necessary.

And so the list could go on. The Royal Family – primarily, of course, the Queen herself – is served by many hundreds of people designated Members of the Household, from the ecclesiastical and medical households to a whole separate household for Scotland. It is a mammoth operation. But we should not forget one further group of professionals in constant attendance, not designated Members of the Household and usually educated at places far removed from the playing fields of Eton: the security officers provided by the Special Branch of Her Majesty's Constabulary. In many cases, notably that of Prince Charles's long-serving 'shadow', John Maclean, a friendship is established as intimate, discreet and down-to-earth as any a Royal personage will ever know.

Anthony Holden

The Royal Workload

The chart shows the number of engagements undertaken by each member of the Royal Family during two separate years, 1979 and 1982, a total of 1,840 and 2,188 respectively.

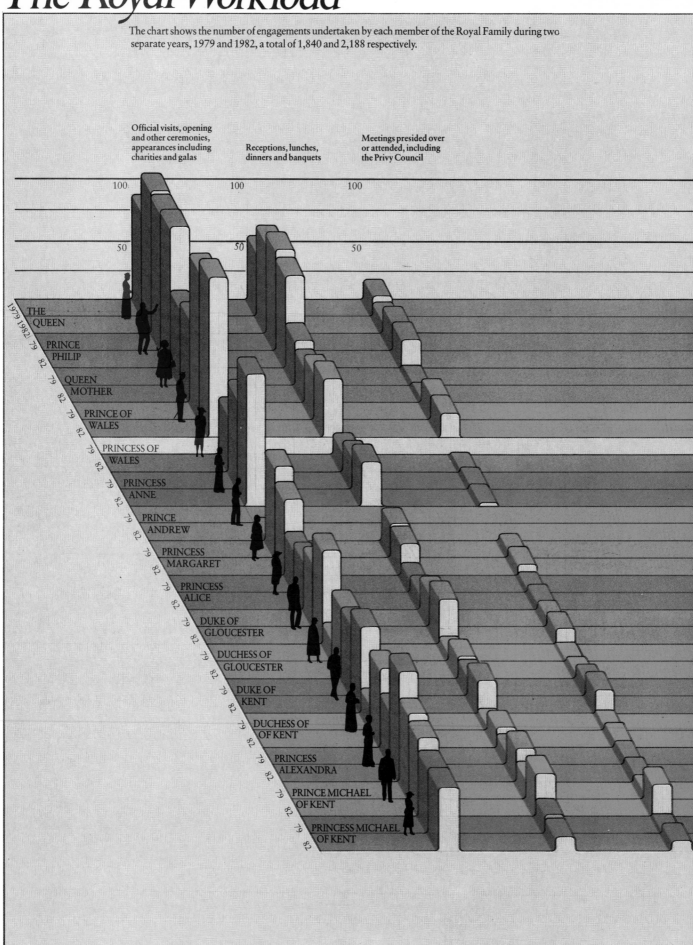

Official visits, opening and other ceremonies, appearances including charities and galas

Receptions, lunches, dinners and banquets

Meetings presided over or attended, including the Privy Council

100   100   100

50   50   50

1979 1982

THE QUEEN
PRINCE PHILIP
QUEEN MOTHER
PRINCE OF WALES
PRINCESS OF WALES
PRINCESS ANNE
PRINCE ANDREW
PRINCESS MARGARET
PRINCESS ALICE
DUKE OF GLOUCESTER
DUCHESS OF GLOUCESTER
DUKE OF KENT
DUCHESS OF OF KENT
PRINCESS ALEXANDRA
PRINCE MICHAEL OF KENT
PRINCESS MICHAEL OF KENT

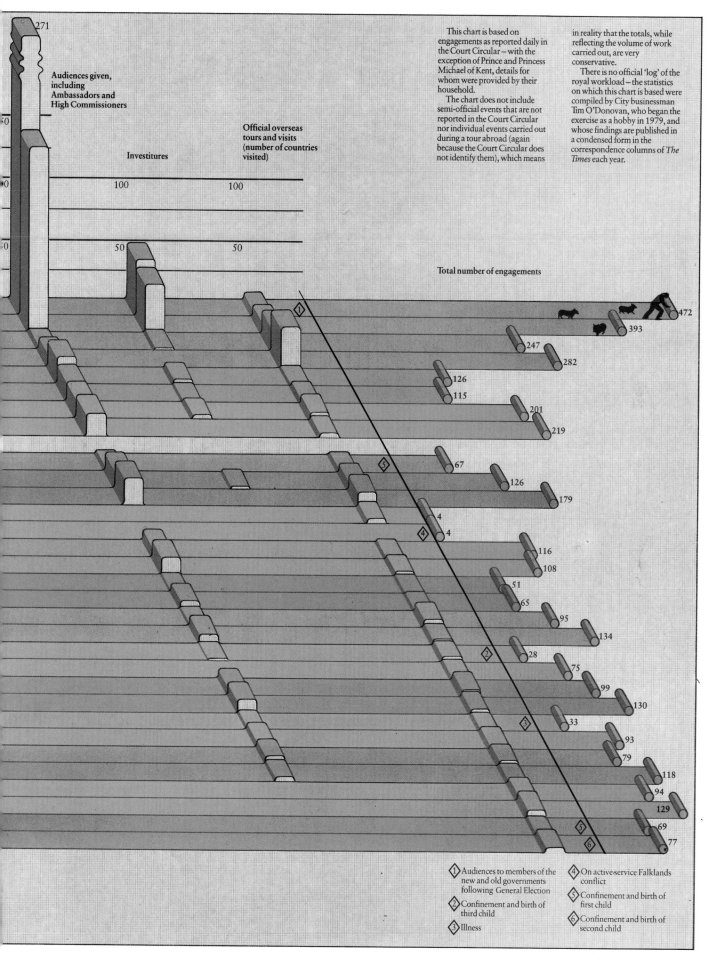

271

Audiences given,
including
Ambassadors and
High Commissioners

Investitures

Official overseas
tours and visits
(number of countries
visited)

100

100

50

50

This chart is based on
engagements as reported daily in
the Court Circular – with the
exception of Prince and Princess
Michael of Kent, details for
whom were provided by their
household.

The chart does not include
semi-official events that are not
reported in the Court Circular
nor individual events carried out
during a tour abroad (again
because the Court Circular does
not identify them), which means

in reality that the totals, while
reflecting the volume of work
carried out, are very
conservative.

There is no official 'log' of the
royal workload – the statistics
on which this chart is based were
compiled by City businessman
Tim O'Donovan, who began the
exercise as a hobby in 1979, and
whose findings are published in
a condensed form in the
correspondence columns of The
Times each year.

Total number of engagements

472

393

247

282

126

115

201

219

67

126

179

4

4

116

108

51

65

95

134

28

75

99

130

33

93

79

118

94

129

69

77

① Audiences to members of the
new and old governments
following General Election

② Confinement and birth of
third child

③ Illness

④ On active service Falklands
conflict

⑤ Confinement and birth of
first child

⑥ Confinement and birth of
second child

ACKNOWLEDGEMENTS

The writers

Anthony Holden
Freelance journalist, author and *Sunday Express Magazine* columnist. He can be heard weekly on Radio 4's *In The Air* and wrote and presented the major BBC TV documentary on foreign royalty, *The Men Who Would Be King*. His biography, *Charles, Prince of Wales*, was a huge bestseller.

Ronald Payne
Former *Sunday Telegraph* diplomatic correspondent. Now a freelance journalist and author of several books, including the best-selling *The Carlos Complex* (with Christopher Dobson).

Andrew Duncan
Freelance journalist and author who contributes prolifically to leading publications on both sides of the Atlantic. His books include *The Reality of Monarchy*, and *Money Rush*.

Tom Davies
Formerly Pendennis on *The Observer* and author of *Merlin the Magician and the Pacific Coast Highway*. Currently working on his second novel.

Lynn Barber
Freelance journalist, broadcaster and author of four books, the latest of which is *The Heyday of Natural History*.

Jane McKerron
Former *New Statesman* staffer and *Sunday Telegraph* columnist, now a freelance journalist and racing correspondent of *Tatler*.

Gay Search
Freelance journalist who has presented programmes for both BBC TV and ITV and is a regular panellist on Radio 4's *The News Quiz*. Her books include *Variations on Wayne Sleep* and *Surviving Divorce: A Handbook for Men*, published in 1983.

Peter Lewis
Author and critic whose books include *George Orwell – the Road to 1984* and *The Prince of Wales Wedding Day*. Winner of the 1978 British Press Award for International Reporting and former literary editor of the *Daily Mail*, he is now a freelance journalist.

Brian Masters
Author of several books including *The Dukes, The Life of Marie Corelli, Georgina, Duchess of Devonshire* and most recently, *The Great Hostesses*. Literary reviewer for *Books and Bookmen*, the *Spectator* and *The Standard*.

Shirley Lowe
Freelance journalist and former Editor of *Over 21*. Author of *Nouveau Poor* (with Barbara Griggs) and a member of the Policy Advisory Committee on Sexual Offences to the Criminal Law Revision Committee at the Home Office.

Celia Haddon
Freelance journalist and author whose books include *Great Days and Jolly Days*, and *The Sunday Times Book of Body Maintenance*.

Yvonne Roberts
Freelance journalist who worked in television for seven years, covering the Middle East for *Weekend World* and social issues for *The London Programme*. She is currently working on a new book.

Pauline Peters
Assistant Editor of the *Sunday Express Magazine*. Formerly a freelance journalist, she was also a writer on *The Sunday Times*.

Deborah Moggach
Author of five novels: *You Must Be Sisters, Close to Home, A Quiet Drink, Hot Water Man* and *Porky*. A former theatre critic and book reviewer, she is now a freelance journalist.

Stephen Clackson
Assistant Editor of the *Sunday Express Magazine* and a former News Editor and Assistant Editor of *The Evening Standard*.

We would like to thank everyone who helped in the preparation of this book, in particular John Haslam of the Buckingham Palace Press Office, and his colleagues who deal with other members of the Royal Family – Colonel Sir Simon Bland, Sir Richard Buckley, Miss Mona Mitchell, Major John Griffin, and John Barratt; also Tim O'Donovan, the Express Newspapers library and the Tasiemka Archives.

Picture credits

We would like to thank all the photographers and photographic agencies whose pictures help bring A Week In The Life Of The Royal Family so vividly into focus. In particular we would like to give special mention to Jennifer Beeston, Julian Calder, Richard Cooke, John Garrett, Martyn Goddard, Tim Graham, Graham Harrison, Neill Meneer, Patrick Ward, Darryl Williams and Jerry Young who worked with our writers through the crucial week, often surmounting considerable logistical difficulties. We are also grateful to Barratts, Ron Bell/Press Association, Jim Bennett/ Camera Press, Birmingham Post, Tom Blau/Camera Press, British Transport Films, CLI/Keystone, Bryn Colton/Camera Press, Coventry Evening Telegraph, Country Life, Anwar Hussein, Jack Knight, The Law Society, Patrick Lichfield/Camera Press, Peter Moxon, Norman Parkinson/ Camera Press, Don Parry (artwork), Photo-Mayo Ltd, Press Association, Rediffusion of Crawley, Rex Features, Ken Rimell/ The News (Portsmouth), Brian Seed, Snowdon/ Camera Press, Donald Southern and Universal Pictorial Press.

Picture credits

Endpapers, front: Menneer, back: Cooke. Title page - Graham. Contents page - Seed.
4 All Menneer.
6/7 Artwork: Parry.
8 Menneer.

12 Graham.
14 Harrison.
16/17 Clockwise from top left hand corner Hussein, Hussein, Hussein, Hussein, Garrett, Graham (main picture), Graham, Graham.
18 Moxon.
20/21 All Menneer.
22/23 Menneer.
24/25 (main picture) Menneer, others, left to right, Menneer, Menneer, Press Association.
26/27 Both Harrison.
28/29 Both Harrison.
30/31 Both Moxon.
32/33 Top row left Hussein, left Menneer, botton row left Hussein, all others Graham.
34 Cooke.
36/37 All Cooke.
38/39 All Cooke.
40/41 Garrett.
42/43 All Menneer.
44/45 Main picture Rediffusion/Crawley, below Rimell/The News (Portsmouth).
46/47 Top row all Graham; main picture Cooke; below left to right Hussein, Graham, Graham.
48 Ward.
50/51 Camera Press.
52/53 All Ward.
54/55 All Garrett except top right The Law Society.
56/57 Top and middle left Ward, bottom left both British Transport Films with insert Ward, top right Colton/Camera Press, bottom right Ward.
58/59 Ward.
60/61 All Ward.
62/63 All Ward except bottom right Photo-Mayo Ltd.
64 Graham.
66/67 Graham.
68 Main picture Graham,

below left to right Bennett/ Camera Press, Barratts, Barratts, Barretts.
70/71 Left above Hussein, below CLI/Keystone, main picture CLI/Keystone.
72 Main picture Bennett/ Camera Press, top right Bennett/Camera Press, below Calder.
74/75 Main picture Hussein, bottom left Hussein, bottom right Graham.
76/77 Bennett/Camera Press.
78/79 Rex Features.
80/81 All Garrett.
82/83 All Garrett.
84 Harrison.
86/87 All Harrison.
88/89 Top left Harrison, main picture Knight.
90/91 Main picture Graham, others, clockwise from top left, Graham, Graham, Country Life, Graham, Country Life, Graham, Country Life, Country Life, Graham.
92 Graham.
94/95 Top left Graham, main picture Hussein, bottom right Hussein.
96/97 Main picture Graham, top left Graham, top right Coventry Evening Telegraph.
98/99 Main picture Harrison, inset top Southern, inset below Southern.
100 Beeston.
102/103 Main picture Beeston, top left Beeston, top right Young.
104/105 All Beeston.
106 Williams.
108/109 All Goddard.
110/111 All Goddard.
112 Young.
114/115 Young.
116/117 Main picture Young, above Beeston.
118/119 Both Young.

120 All Williams.
122/123 Both Williams.
124/125 All Williams.
126/127 All Williams.
128 Menneer.
130/131 All Harrison.
132/133 All Calder.
134/135 Main picture Harrison, right Garrett.
136/137 Both Garrett.
138 Inset Bell/Press Association.
140/141 Top row left to right Camera Press, Hussein, Parkinson/Camera Press, bottom row both Hussein.
142/143 Top row Lichfield/Camera Press, Snowdon/Camera Press, Crickmay, Camera Press, below Graham, Snowdon/ Camera Press.
144 Main picture Camera Press, inserts left to right Camera Press, Universal, Camera Press.
146/147 Top row left to right Graham, Blau/ Camera Press, below both Hussein.
148/149 Top Camera Press, below Graham.
150/151 Artwork: Parry.

Picture co-ordination Rae Lewis.

153